REALECONOMIK

GRIGORY YAVLINSKY

REALECONOMIK

The Hidden
Cause of the Great Recession
(and How to Avert the Next One)

Translated from the Russian by
Antonina W. Bouis

Yale
UNIVERSITY PRESS
NEW HAVEN & LONDON

Set in Galliard type by Integrated Publishing Solutions,
Grand Rapids, Michigan.

Printed in the United States of America.

Library of Congress Cataloging-in-Publication Data

Iavlinskii, G. (Grigorii)
Realeconomik : the hidden cause of the great recession (and how to
avert the next one) / Grigory Yavlinsky ; translated from the Russian by
Antonina W. Bouis.
    p. cm.
Includes bibliographical references and index.
ISBN 978-0-300-15910-3 (hardback)
1. Wealth—Moral and ethical aspects. 2.Recessions. 3. Capitalism.
4. Bank failures. 5. Financial crises—Prevention. 6. Global Financial
Crisis, 2008–2009. I. Title.
HB835.I28 2011
330.9′0511—dc22   2011012017

A catalogue record for this book is available from the British Library.

This paper meets the requirements of ANSI/NISO Z39.48-1992
(Permanence of Paper).

10 9 8 7 6 5 4 3 2 1

To my children

CONTENTS

P R E F A C E

There is no crisis for people who play Bach.
—FROM A CONVERSATION AT THE CONSERVATORY

It would have been pointless to write a book like this just three years ago—one simply couldn't hope for a positive response. But the situation is different now, largely because of two changes. The first is the financial crisis of 2007–2009, which made at least some of the educated public more interested in understanding the underlying fundamental problems of the current world economy.

Second, and this could be more significant, the current debate on economic policy of U.S. President Barack Obama's administration provides more room and opportunities for serious discussion than before.

Before these changes occurred, any debate on such issues would in principle have been consigned to oblivion, so there was only one option—to wait for the opportune moment.

The title and subtitle, *Realeconomik: The Hidden Cause of the Great Recession (and How to Avert the Next One)*, reflect the central idea of this book: the cause of the crisis is that at the core, modern capitalism is concerned with money and power, not ideals, morals, or principles. I use the word *Realeconomik* as an analogue to Realpolitik, a pejorative term for politics that masquerades as practicality while in fact comprising the cynicism, coercion, and amorality of Machiavellian principles.

Contemporary economists might not accept some of the ideas proposed in this book. I could not have published these ideas even in the first half of 2008 without being considered at best retrograde or at worst an ignoramus. Even now I have little hope that the opinions of contemporary trendsetters in economics and business have changed. However, it is possible that what is variously described as the "Great Recession of the early twenty-first century" or the "longest U.S. slump since the 1930s" will make at least some of these people consider seriously the argument of this book.

Unfortunately, the reasoning you will find here has become unfashionable. In the 1950s, when the world was still extricating itself from the ruins of World War II, the ideas I wish to discuss were more a part of public discussion. Today, many will find them politically incorrect, if not seditious. An entire generation of Western politicians, businessmen, and economists has come of age without ever thinking seriously about the relationship between morality and economics or ethics and politics.

If we turn to eastern Europe, in particular early in the post-Soviet age, such discussions were out of the question. It was generally accepted that business should be measured only by profits. Politicians who succeeded communist-era leaders (and who largely had been a part of the communist ruling class) proclaimed the transition from totalitarianism to market democracy yet actually adopted the most unprincipled and cynical view of the nature of politics, driven by the all-encompassing conviction (learned in their communist past) that in a market capitalist society only profits mattered—the central idea of Realeconomik.

In this book I do not seek to make any moral judgments: I aim instead to be descriptive and analytical. My goal is not to moralize, but rather to indicate those areas that are usually not discussed in public—to write what many people think but may prefer to keep to themselves. I have tried to be more or less impartial, though one may perceive judgment behind many of my words. I have no intention of condemning anybody as mean or immoral: in no way do I consider myself a man who has the right to judge my fellow human beings. Anyway, that's not my task.

I aim to formulate a number of thoughts about what I perceive to be the underlying causes of the global economic, moral, and political crisis at the beginning of the twenty-first century. Testing some of the ideas contained in this book will surely require several years of solid academic work. Nevertheless, I accepted the kind offer of Yale University Press to publish it now, because time moves so swiftly in our modern world that I feel the urgency to state clearly the things that I believe to be crucial to understanding the events unfolding before our eyes.

The underlying premise of this book is that the nature of the Great Recession is not only economic—or perhaps not even attributable mainly to economic factors. Neither is it the product of mere complacency and negligence of duty on the part of authorities and top-level managers in the private sector, as some experts insist. Rather, the underlying fundamentals and causes go deeper—to such things as general rules of society and the logic to which they are subject, encompassing the issues of individual and social values, moral guidance, and public control, as well as their evolution over the past several decades. These issues are much more serious and have a greater impact on economic performance than is customarily believed.

Academic researchers and governmental decision makers should not lose sight of the fact that even comparatively sophisticated ways of responding to this crisis, as proposed by many, such as writing new, stringent rules, exercising more public control over their enforcement, imposing taxes on some kinds of financial operations, and the like will not resolve fundamental problems, which are not simply economic. Far less will be achieved by simply "pouring money on the crisis," even if it is accompanied by exposing the banking secrets of thousands of officials and businessmen.

There are no ready-made solutions to these problems. However, I hope this book will provide a fresh perspective for anyone concerned about another bursting bubble, persistently high unemployment, the "new normal" (economic stagnation in a low-growth, low-inflation environment), financial volatility, sharply rising poverty rates (even in industrialized nations such as the United States), and social unrest, or the possibility of something more catastrophic.

My book is not a clarion call to change everything instantly. At the same time, the ideas discussed here could and should become the cornerstone of modern policies in developed countries that could help overcome certain disturbing political, economic, and social developments of the past twenty-five years.

I have structured this book to include a number of ideas and observations that reveal the key traits of the modern Western economic and political system from the perspective of various changes of the past two or three decades, both in the essence and character of business activities and in their political and ideological underpinnings. Those changes can tell us much about the global economic decline.

I am ready to accept criticism, as some shortcomings of this book are obvious to me, too. However, the urgency of the problem persuaded me not to let perfection be the enemy of the good. Comprehension of the key provisions should not require extensive scholarly references or an array of empirical evidence.

It is difficult to talk about the economy from the perspective of morality, as the very concept of morality seems to be devoid of established content, is subject to broad interpretation, and is often rather elusive. But those difficulties seem insufficient reason to exclude morality from economic analysis and research. It is essential to treat the issue of morality seriously and extensively to provide a meaningful perspective for economic processes and their consequences, especially in the framework of long-term analysis.

I realize that treating moral sense as an economic phenomenon is a complex enterprise sure to be widely challenged, and I address this subject extensively elsewhere in the book. Nevertheless, I must begin with the premise that there exists a code of simple and well-known, almost universal, informal rules of behavior. These rules are essential to the efficient functioning of market mechanisms and need to be constantly maintained, if not enforced, by public institutions. Consequently, public neglect of these rules in business, as well as in regulating activities, may lead—and to a large extent has already led—to serious deficiencies in economic mechanisms, first and foremost in the financial sector.

I believe this premise is of utmost importance, and that may excuse my desire to share with the readers my personal impressions and findings. The latter originate not only from my research but also from daily experience of mixing with people who consider the relation of politics and business to morality an issue unworthy of serious consideration. The viewpoint of these people reflects the cynical attitudes common in the West, and it also represents a psychological vestige of the hypocritical totalitarian past in the Eastern Bloc countries. This worst-of-both-worlds combination often produces the atmosphere I call Realeconomik: undisguised cynicism that can lead to lawlessness, corruption, and even violence as a means to resolve political and economic disagreements.

Certainly I understand the difference and draw a clear line between personal codes of behavior and the much more complex ethics in public policy. Nevertheless, that line is neither absolute nor insurmountable: a politician who maintains ethical principles in his private life is likelier to implement them in politics, though the degree to which he can do so may be limited by the results achievable. If sticking to principles dooms a policy to failure, that policy is flawed; achieving positive results without compromising principle is the true art of politics, an art sadly neglected.

In this book I hope to demonstrate the need to rearrange our economic mindset to allow more room for values and guidelines to govern the behavior of economic agents. If I succeed in drawing public attention to this need, I will consider my mission fulfilled.

REALECONOMIK

Introduction

At first nobody can diagnose a serious illness. However, by the time everyone can see it, it's too late.

— EXPERIENCED PHYSICIAN

The financial meltdown of 2007–2009 prompted me to write this book. While there have been lots of theories and discussions about the crisis, they primarily centered on the surface issues, or those not far beneath. Causes have been discussed, too, but largely the immediate and simple ones, which explain many things but not all that matter. Being an observer of developments rather than an interested participant in stock exchange gambling, I longed for answers to questions more about the deeper meaning of market disorders than about how particular markets function (and malfunction), and I couldn't find answers that satisfied me.

But the crisis served as a convenient starting point. The questions it raises are not new—they have been in the air for quite some time, and every now and then they were raised for consideration. The global economic slowdown brought them to light—probably for a brief time only, as they will again fall off the radar of scholars, practicing businessmen, and politicians once the Great Recession is past and stability resumes.

So I have no intention to present yet another personal view of "hot issues" about the global slump; rather, I think of this book as an attempt to find answers to the bigger questions elicited over the past several decades, questions that will confront us for a long time to come. But because the crisis triggered my curiosity, the first set of questions relates to its character and its causes.

Standard economics textbooks describe business cycles of various natures and durations, of various degrees of severity and corresponding consequences. Cycles happen, and there is nothing unusual about them. But if that's the case, why is there so much fuss about this particular instance of financial market disorder—why has it been ascribed nearly catastrophic dimensions?[1] If, on the contrary, this case is so particular and special, why has it been addressed with the standard set of policy measures regularly used in business cycles?[2]

If everybody agrees that the reasons for this crisis are not confined to cyclical factors, then what are those extraordinary reasons? As no one has been able to provide plausible explanations aside from vague "policy failure," there must have been quite a lot of these unusual "failures" to produce a convulsion of such magnitude. If so, why did economic and monetary authorities, market regulators, rating agencies, and other experts make so many wrong choices?

If the gravity of the situation with American subprime mortgage loans was apparent to professionals more than a year before the dramatic decline in the stock markets began in the summer of 2008, why was it allowed ultimately to develop into a freeze in international financial relations and a perceptible recession in many parts of the world economy?

Speaking more generally, why do all those malfunctions, declines, and crashes happen when they do, and why do they almost always come as a surprise to recognized economic gurus? (Of course, many experts maintain post facto that they foresaw everything that occurred and even more, but such claims are no more useful than the observation that a broken watch indicates the correct time twice a day.)

Extending the inquiry still further, why do as many elements in the operations of a market economy remain mysterious as was the case a hundred years ago or more, even though economic theory has in the past century far overtaken economy and business in complexity? Why do stock market analysts, drawing on constant improvements in technical and fundamental analysis software, still resemble astrologers, with the accuracy of their forecasts depending mostly on the scope of possible interpretations? If the financial authorities are in possession of various tools to regulate credit, price movements, investments, and consumer activity with mathematical accuracy, why does it transpire that those tools fail when needed most, because computations are made on the premise that most variables do not vary? What is the practical value of tools that fail worst when needed most? And why must investors and taxpayers bear the cost of their never-ending updates?

Other questions offer no evident or convincing answers. In developed economies even severe recessions are rarely accompanied nowadays by deep reductions in revenues and volume of business activity: two-digit negative growth rates for leading market economies have come to be viewed as largely theoretical scenarios. Inflation, which devalues savings and fixed incomes, as a rule does not exceed a few percentage points and, if we are to believe statistics, falls almost to zero in adverse market conditions. However, if this is the case, it would be logical to assume that losses by some people should be offset, even if at a discount, by gains for other people. If a large number of people, companies, and even entire branches of industry and areas of the economy incur extensive revenue losses and asset impairments during crises, then these losses should result in significant gains for other people—yet for some reason we never hear of such profits.

So if there are no winners, or virtually no winners, doesn't this mean that precrisis estimates of aggregate revenues and assets had been artificially inflated as a result of incorrect or fraudulent data? If so, why do not more experts decry such grossly incorrect estimates? Why do they instead unfailingly speak of the coming recovery and again advise people where to invest whatever money they have left after the last meltdown, instead of addressing the issue of what went wrong before and during the crisis, and whom the people who suffered losses might blame (aside, of course, from themselves)?

Searching for answers to these and other similar questions, I couldn't find a consensus in the general discourse. However, if there is no visible cause, then there must be a hidden one. Certainly one can come up with various explanations, including quite elaborate and exotic ones—intervention by extraterrestrial forces, say. But I think there is a single reason that sheds light on all my questions. It looks like a hidden cause because few people are inclined to see it or talk about it. Most are reluctant to dwell on the subject because it leads to conclusions that are unflattering at best.

But before turning to this subject, I'd like to make some other explanatory remarks. As I said earlier, the slump has brought to light many unpleasant truths. Most of them, however, have deeper roots and implications.

The alarming signs and signals are not unique to the crisis but raise much bigger issues.

So I could not help asking myself questions of yet another nature.

What is the modern meaning of utility, which is one of the cornerstones of the mainstream theory of modern capitalism, and what is the meaning of the human needs that represent an essential condition for economic goods to possess utility? How should we define utility, and who is in the position to do the defining? Why do we have to buy a certain set of goods and services, and how could we know their actual utility and their costs of production? Who actually sets the price for all these goods and services, and how is the price set? Do we really have to pay it, and if so, why? And what, under current conditions, is the real meaning of the notion of productivity, which is also central and essential to the modern theory of capitalism? How can it be measured, and does it bear any practical sense?

Private property, we are told, is the basis and the most essential element of a capitalist market economy. If there really has been a "manager revolution," allowing executives de facto to prevent the formal owners of industrial assets from disposing of their property and also the income that it generates, thus stripping any practical meaning from the formal right to private property, the question arises: Why is there so little debate on this issue, and why are no allowances made for this revolution when practical policies are proposed to invigorate economic growth? Why is it presumed generally that firms and banks act as if they are being operated for the benefit of their shareholders, maximizing their current and future value?

The transition to a capitalist market economy of former Eastern Bloc countries added greater social complexity; society was divided along new lines, with greater gaps between strata. That development posed yet another set of questions. What laws and rules govern the distribution of income and property under modern capitalism? Why do new gaps arise for no obvious or convincing reason, and how does that inequality correlate with the notion of fairness and justice—if indeed those qualities are to be applied to the subject?

Why did the financial sector grow to such size and complexity? What lies beneath this expansion? Have financial technologies made some real progress, such that financial products have become more convenient or safe? Or maybe what has happened is a kind of intellectual alchemy, bordering on deceit? Why is it that amid an impressive flood of financial services being advertised, there are so few people who boast that they have benefited from them?

The mantra of much present-day economic thinking is that the new economy emerging to replace its industrial predecessor is knowledge-based and oriented toward innovation. But questions remain unanswered here as well: What do the innovations accomplish, and how do they relate to the welfare of society, to the public interest? What is understood by the public interest, and who evaluates and formulates it? Who makes money from "intellectual innovation"? Who pays for it, and why? And how does this transaction affect the distribution of income and property on a global scale? What basic logic, if any, governs these processes?

It may seem not logical, but thinking over these and other more fundamental issues—as well as considering what lessons might be drawn from the slide into the Great Recession—has brought me to a single conclusion: when no clear visible reasons explain a phenomenon, hidden causes may exist. Perhaps the hidden cause is too complex and arcane to discover, but perhaps it is right beneath the surface, willfully ignored rather than obscure.

Now I come to the topic that forms the nexus of this whole book, and to the main message that I hope my readers will take away. To have a viable, effective, and efficient economic system, we must reject the mindset that drives Realeconomik, the notion that "Homo economicus" bases his judgments on purely rational, narrowly economic considerations.

The ability to secure the information essential for making economically rational decisions is limited. Moreover, this limitation becomes more pronounced as economic life becomes more complex, as the utility of goods and services offered to consumers becomes less self-evident and requires more and more expertise. On the contrary, a greater role arises for irrational considerations, like passions and desires, and for accepted rules and values, motives and constraints that constitute what we define as ethics or morality.

These rules and values and the motives and constraints that arise from them are rarely granted prime importance in discussions of economic behavior, and often they are simply dismissed as irrelevant. However, they provide a simple and plausible explanation for much around us and answer many questions I have raised.

The financial decline that unfolded in 2007–2009 has numerous contributing factors, some related to business cycles, some to structural changes in the financial sector, and some to wrong decisions by relevant authorities or private institutions. Nevertheless, as I hope to show, many questions stemming from this crisis will remain unanswered if we stay within the realm of analysis of relevant decisions as right or mistaken, competent or poorly worked out, ignoring their ethical and social background. To avert yet another outbreak of financial instability, we should not limit ourselves to the mere indication of policy failures or incorrect risk assessments. We must confront the spread across the financial sector and related industries of tolerance for dubious and overtly misleading practices. We must hold governments and lawmakers accountable when they yield to financial sector lobbies and hand out undue favors. We must not tolerate the irresponsible indifference by authorities and experts on whose opinion they rely to a dangerous accumulation of risks in the financial system.

Moreover, the "hidden" factor of moral weakness, when put in the right perspective, may help to give a coherent picture of the inner logic of modern capitalism and its current evolution, as well as a satisfactory explanation of the dangerous changes in the economic world over the past several decades.

The structure of Western economies has undergone a visible and possibly irreversible shift in favor of the financial sector, while increasing the share of the costs of various intellectual (or pseudointellectual, as is often the case) components in the products of other sectors. This shift may have certain objective and natural driving forces behind it, like the increasing importance of knowledge for production activities, or the preponderance of complex links between economic agents requiring greater specialization. But in parallel to those forces we can see business in these sectors becoming less transparent, increasingly seducing those engaged in it into misleading and deceitful behavior. We can also see people in these sectors using their advantageous positions to extract royalty payments from their clients as fees for intellectual assets created by past generations, which they have groundlessly privatized. Finally, they openly manipulate consumer psychology, using not only aggressive and coercive advertising but blatant deception disguised as mysterious "innovations." All this has been made possible by the passivity of politicians and the open collaboration by members of the intellectual elite.

Ethical considerations also come into play, as I hope to prove, in the modern trend in international economic policy of dividing the world into zones characterized by great differences in the levels of economic and social development. This policy progresses in parallel with the much-heralded economic globalization. While certain objective reasons exist for such division —the importance of starting positions, for example, and the difficulty of great leaps forward—it is impossible to ignore the factors directly related to morality. Too often the West rejects any bridging of the gap between rich and poor nations, insisting, for example, on strict enforcement of "intellectual property rights."

Another related topic on which I shall dwell is the renewed attempt to use ideological differences and preferences to divide the world into privileged and discriminated-against nations. Again, one cannot deny the differences between countries with deep democratic traditions and those characterized by authoritarian rule, rigid social hierarchy, and a low priority for individual rights and freedoms. But the tendency to separate black sheep from white ones globally smacks of an attempt to revitalize the dubious moral agendas of past centuries, which presumed the duty of the world aristocracy ("the white man's burden") to impose "civilized" attitudes on other nations. More often than not that "duty" was a pretext for pursuit of imperial and private interests. The same could be said of the recent tendency to construe multiculturalism as "the conflict of civilizations."

Finally, and most important, basic moral attitudes have shifted significantly in the business context—a shift that seems an attempt to discard moral codes altogether. The new regime would make it theoretically impossible to assess business activities according to the criteria of public interest and social utility; only the illegal—criminal black markets, for example, would be construed as "immoral." This tendency is best characterized by the reasoning that profitable sales by definition denote the satisfaction of consumer needs, which (again by definition) makes such business activities socially useful, or (if one likes it that way) ethically justified.

Here, too, such a line of thinking is not altogether groundless: if money is the only measurement of utility, no external value-based criteria can be applied. However, that approach is ethical nihilism, a lightly veiled rejection of any role for morality in economic decisions.

Morality not only has a place in daily activities involving exchange, saving, investment, the production of goods, and other basic economic activities, its role is as important as the laws maintained by governments. In fact, my experience convinces me that law imposed by the state works more or less satisfactorily according to the degree to which it is reinforced by the momentum of daily life in accord with principles spontaneously developed over time by societies as they survive and evolve. Among these principles is morality.

It is also important to make clear from the beginning that I use the word *morality* not in the simple sense of personal moral qualities or ethical standards, but rather in the sense of the guiding principles by which a society as a whole is governed. I am not a preacher, and I leave the denunciation of individual vices and the praise of individual virtues to theologians and philosophers. One person's personal greed poses little threat to a culture, but a society or a government ruled by greed, which privileges self-interest as a natural and universal phenomenon, is the focus of my concern. In the context of this book, morality is something social and systemic, the underlying causes of which are partly political, partly economic, and partly historical. These causes are also largely invisible because they rely not on conscious effort but on something a little bit below consciousness—an inclination, shaped by prevailing conditions of life, to see things in a particular way.

The topics raised in chapters 2 ("Capitalism, the Market, and Morality"), 3 ("Shifts in the Global Economy of the 1980s–2010 and Changes in the Moral and Psychological Climate"), and 4 ("International Relations, 1980s–2008: Putting Self-Interest First") I hope offer quite original approaches to problems of economic policy and international relations. Certainly no systematized analysis has ever been conducted linking issues of practicality in policy and business activity with morality and its influence on daily decisions. Many of the ideas and characterizations in the chapter on the Russian economic crisis also reflect my own vision of the subject, born of personal experience. Finally, I considered it my task to establish logical links among a wide range of topics and key points that were overlooked or shortchanged by other authors. If, for example, my attempt to establish a direct link between the proliferation of the so-called new economy and a higher risk of deviating trends on financial markets invites further discussion, I will consider my work worthwhile.

In this book I try to infuse economic thinking with a sense of morality, in part as a model for economics and economic journalism. I introduce the terms *intellectual (asset) rent payment* and *historical rent payment* to help better explain modern pricing mechanisms. These mechanisms are part of the barrier that threatens to divide forever the developed economies from poorer countries.

I shall try to answer the questions I have posed, though I recognize that no one can see more than a fragment of the picture of the evolution of the modern market economy. But the attempt to find answers to these questions has brought me to consider more seriously the role of moral standards for the future of capitalist economy.

Moreover, if we pursue these questions to their logical conclusion, some even more fundamental questions arise. What rules of behavior should we follow in business, and which of these rules are practically feasible? What guidelines should we consider for selecting them and attempting to implement these rules? What should serve as underlying principles, and how is any of this connected to morality? And how should we treat the condition of the world as we find it—as something inevitable and beyond our control, or as something we can change through concentrated and coordinated actions?

Naturally, these questions go far beyond the conventional scope of economic research and analysis. Moreover, they may sound metaphysical to those who consider them appropriate only to religious belief, not to economic research. Even if we look at the questions as matters of political choice, they cannot finally be answered satisfactorily by any individual scholar or, for that matter, by any political group. Nevertheless, I consider it my duty to try to provoke a debate on these fundamental issues, as I am convinced that the time has come to consider them seriously and to begin, at last, to seek answers that are applicable to the world as it stands today.

I

Developments in the Global Economy

Everyone thinks only of himself and no one about the common cause.

—LUDWIG GERHARDT

The Economic Crisis: A General Impression

In the spring of 2009, when I read newspaper coverage of worldwide economic developments and tried to formulate my own impression, I caught myself thinking that any evaluation of past events can be neither simple nor unambiguous. A variety of shocks, changes, and phenomena appear to occur simultaneously in different dimensions of economic life. Thus many descriptions and interpretations of contemporary economic developments can be found every day in the media, but none of them provides an exhaustive picture of the situation as a whole.

Most important, however, as I acquainted myself more and more with media coverage of the news related to economy and business, I developed a strangely ambivalent sensation that despite a strong consensus about the state of the economy in the industrialized world, many elements, including the underlying causes of the crisis, remained unexplored.

On the one hand, if we view individual economic factors in isolation, nothing has happened that contradicts established wisdom about the nature and internal workings of a market economy. While the scale of the recent disorder is unusually large and its consequences may be extraordinarily serious, all the phenomena currently designated *global economic crisis* have been observed repeatedly in history, even comparatively recently, though in significantly different combinations and sequences. The dependencies that triggered the chain of events in 2007–2009 in the American economy and subsequently globally had been well known to a broad range of specialists. Anyone following the world economy over the past thirty years, for example, would be able to place any aspect of recent events in the context of similar phenomena observed during that span. That such analogues exist tells us that the financial disorder of 2007–2009 should not be portrayed as some turning point in the history of capitalism, as a signal of the impending demise of "financial capitalism," as some politicians (including Chancellor Angela Merkel of Germany and President Nicolas Sarkozy of France) proclaimed in the wake of the downturn.

It could be claimed, in fact, that the issues raised by the recent troubles —variously described as a financial meltdown, a global economic decline, a crisis of modern market capitalism, the longest U.S. slump since the 1930s, or the Great Recession of the early twenty-first century—are not particularly complicated. The manifestations of the disarray are obvious, from the financial ordeals faced by credit institutions that allowed their long-term financial stability to be undermined by risk, to the dip in demand and production that threatens many companies in the manufacturing sector with bankruptcy, to the hopeless jobs picture in parts of the developed world, such as in Spain, where unemployment reached a devastating 20 percent. Judged from this perspective, nothing fundamentally new is anticipated in the short term: even though predictions on the aftermath and possible repercussions of the recession differ substantially, pretentious statements that the world is "irreversibly changed" must be attributed to journalistic license.

At the same time, however, the numerous interpretations of the nature of this crisis—and, accordingly, its causes and possible consequences—do raise some issues. I will consider these issues in more detail in due course. The most important one, however, is that despite an apparent recognition of the development of pernicious trends in the financial sector in particular and in the economy as a whole, no one—first and foremost the financial authorities—managed to prevent these trends from snowballing or to channel them into comparatively safe outlets. A more than detailed description of the developments that preceded the crisis can be found in the final report of the FCIC, so I don't think it necessary to go into particulars here, assuming that its general conclusion that "this financial crisis was avoidable" has been substantiated with convincing evidence. To put it more simply, people ostensibly competent in these areas—in particular those wielding governmental authority—should have noticed and addressed the dangerous buildup of risks in the financial system. These authorities could have urged that financial institutions take appropriate measures to control this buildup, but they apparently decided that such action was unnecessary. In the aftermath, business commentators and analysts have failed to provide a satisfactory explanation why the authorities failed to act.

In fact, trying to figure out why these figures thought it unnecessary to act inspired the thesis that is at the heart of this book: that the stability and efficiency of an economic system depend on more than economic rationale and professional competence. In some cases, individual values and rules of behavior set by public opinion and attitudes—what might succinctly if perhaps somewhat loosely be called morality—determine the course of events in the sphere traditionally regarded as the domain of economic science.

Realeconomik: Logical Buildup to the Unexpected Denouement

From public pronouncements while the crisis unfolded and even more from post-facto comments, it becomes clear that not only did each stage contain the seeds for potential developments, but it virtually predetermined subsequent stages. As I will demonstrate, the destabilization of one sector followed the destabilization of another related sector, in a direct correlation with theoretical rules and economic logic. No one involved can credibly claim that it was impossible to foresee this; nor can any observer have believed that a process would suddenly stop of its own accord at some stage, or that the problems would simply go away. Therefore it is difficult to find a plausible and convincing intellectual explanation why the financial and political authorities failed to take effective measures to counteract the creeping economic weakness. Most important, it is difficult to understand how both the authorities and specialists in macroeconomics and financial markets could have stood by and watched silently for several years or more as the underlying factors setting the stage for the recession matured and assumed larger proportions—the very factors that made the onset of the meltdown inevitable in some form or other. We must search for an explanation that accounts for the psychological, social, and moral dimensions of the decision-making process that allowed the slump to develop.

However strange it may seem, the scale and acuteness of the downturn apparently came as a surprise to the majority of people who by virtue of their activities and duties should have had access to the necessary information and drawn the appropriate conclusions. Debate did not begin about risky business practices, dubious security on loans, and dangerous actions by top management of the world's largest financial institutions until several months after financial markets had started to malfunction. Finally government regulators began to wake up to the purely abstract and manipulative nature of mathematical models in vogue. These models enabled loosely regulated or unregulated financial institutions to abruptly reduce risk assessments of investments and encouraged the issuers of complex financial derivatives to bring to market still newer financial products (like collateralized "packaged loan" bonds, credit default swaps, and so on), which transferred the risks of individual investors to the financial system as a whole. The regulators and corresponding government ministries and departments "suddenly" discovered that the financial sector's ability to resist the destabilizing impact of additional risks is not boundless and can be undermined comparatively quickly. As a result, the inexplicable complacency was abruptly replaced by alarmist calls for rapid action "to save the financial system from immediate collapse."

This process occurred even though, as we shall see, the emergence and unfolding of the crisis could not reasonably be blamed on some unexpected exogenous circumstances impossible to explain within the framework of known rules of market behavior.

Moreover, we now know that people who worked at lower levels of the financial pyramid knew full well that risks and contradictions, some of them directly attributable to their actions, had accrued in the system and would have to be resolved in some way—either through rigid administrative interventions by regulators or through a spontaneous collapse of the structures that had been accumulating the risks.[1]

Mechanics of Meltdown

To substantiate my thesis that every step of the crisis that has been gradually unfolding since 2007 predictably determined its subsequent stages, let me recall its main stages in more detail.

Trouble on the mortgage bond market in the United States started with a declining price growth for real estate serving as the collateral for mortgages issued by banks; these subprime loans in turn served as collateral for mortgage loans packaged as bonds. In other words, the United States was confronted by an understandable and unexceptional event—impairment of collateral resulting from changing market conditions. Admittedly, in light of the trend of two decades during which prices had consistently risen, the decline in price growth and subsequent fall in the price of real estate may not have seemed to be a run-of-the-mill phenomenon. But perpetual price growth, whether in real estate or in energy, contradicts a fundamental market principle: that all prices are subject to corrections. Consequently, market players and regulators had no reason to assume that these prices would not stabilize or regress at some stage, possibly in the immediate future.

As bonds backed by real estate served as the basis for the creation of a number of financial derivatives and also for the emergence of a whole pyramid of credit default swaps (CDS), it was only natural that the collapse of the subprime market did not remain a purely local disturbance but led instead to defaults on payments for a number of securities in the portfolios of major institutional investors, including savings banks, pension funds, and investment companies.[2] One question remains to date unanswered: how did these institutional investors and "analysts" acting on their behalf assess the reliability of investing in these securities? Such losses could be explained by lack of access to information or innocent misjudgment, but as I will show, a more plausible explanation lies in the lack of moral restraints resulting from a lax public attitude and the tacit acceptance by regulating bodies of irresponsible and fraudulent financial practices.

That the impairment of mortgage collateral would trigger a wave of defaults on payments in a long chain of derivatives was an absolutely logical and predictable phenomenon. Three factors led to a crisis of confidence in the banking and more broadly in the financial sector: the significant number of defaults on securities, the inability to determine exactly where the chain of defaults would end, and the inability to ascertain the size of the defaults. Banks may not have known, but could have assumed, that because of impaired assets, huge "holes" had appeared or would soon appear in the balance sheets of their counterparts in financial markets. The banks consequently became increasingly reluctant to make further loans and eager to reduce their potential losses by tightening loan terms. This led to the credit crunch and the introduction of more stringent terms and conditions for borrowers, and in the end higher interest rates on loans for virtually all categories of borrowers.

The resulting rise in interest rates on the interbank market, which is used to determine the final borrower's payments on certain types of loans, led to an increasing number of defaults on consumer loans, including credit card loans, as well as corporate-sector defaults. In certain categories of borrowers—in particular households, which had to a large extent already been classified as unreliable and consequently had no chance to refinance loans through an alternative source—even a comparatively minor tightening of credit conditions triggered defaults on regular loan repayments.

When banks started selling collateral on defaulted loans, they triggered a further plunge in real estate prices and exacerbated instability on the stock market, which in turn adversely affected the reliability of a significant amount of collateral. This led to a vicious circle on the stock market: as more shares serving as collateral for defaulted loans were sold—including forced sales by investors desperate to repay loans and other increasingly expensive obligations, or to pay individual investors, who had decided to exit the market for collective investments—prices fell. The sinking prices in turn provided further motivation for investors to sell shares that were losing value, thus further undermining collateral and fueling the trade in illiquid shares, sending market capitalization lower still.

As a result huge holes appeared on the balance sheets of investment banks and other financial corporations operating as institutional investors that were weighed down by rapidly depreciating assets, the American International Group (AIG) insurance giant being the most vivid example. At the same time, the ability of these corporations to borrow and discharge current obligations contracted critically. These corporations made numerous appeals to the government for financial aid in the form of loans and capital investments. There followed a succession of mergers, the bankruptcy of Lehman Brothers and a number of smaller financial corporations, and an overall reduction in the scale of financial investments, triggering extensive layoffs. These shocks in the financial sector followed a logical progression, culminating in a full-fledged global slowdown.

Such turbulence in the financial sector deepened the negative mindset in the manufacturing sector, which is also understandable and logical. The crisis in the financial sector made it increasingly difficult for manufacturers to take out loans, while their ability to borrow on the stock market was also severely restricted. At the same time, after the collapse of a sizable number of financial assets owned by households either directly or indirectly, consumer demand naturally contracted, with losses to U.S. companies alone running into trillions of dollars. Consequently, first the U.S. economy and then European economies confronted a downturn in demand and were at the same time constrained from further borrowing. The contraction in consumer demand and the subsequent onset of a recession for developed economies was a natural and unavoidable consequence of the disruption in the financial sector. Only the scale and industry-specific nature of the impact could be considered unpredictable; the impact itself was predetermined.

The issue of commodity and energy prices is more complicated. Prices on commodity and energy markets started falling before the financial crunch in the United States and Europe had become acute. Accordingly, the fall in global prices for oil and other fuels, and for metals and chemicals and some other products in the primary sector, was not attributable solely to instability in the financial markets: other factors contributed, including the cyclical nature of pricing on commodity markets. The growing importance of speculative trading on these markets—in particular the huge increase in oil futures, which drove oil prices to inconceivable heights—also ensured that these prices would fall not long after. However, at a certain stage of development in the crisis, fluctuations in the prices of oil and industrial commodities were closely linked to expectations of a recession in the industrial sector of both developed countries and export-driven economies in the developing world.

The drop in commodity and energy prices had an adverse impact on the financial standing of countries that depend on the extraction industries for a large proportion of the economy, including taxes, employment, and export proceeds. Russia, which I will discuss in detail later, is one of the comparatively large economies in this category, together with Brazil, South Africa, Australia, and several others, including to some extent Canada and Norway. However, in general this factor played a positive role for developed economies. Within the overall context of the global crisis, the drop in commodity and energy prices was an ambiguous factor, ultimately fairly minor.

My point in retelling the progress of the world economic decline is to substantiate the thesis presented in the previous section, that the chain of events which led to disarray in financial markets and then to general recession was perfectly logical and predictable. It required no magic insight or heavenly enlightenment to foresee what could be expected next and hence to take necessary action. All that was required of authorities was mere competence and conscientious execution of public duties.

The fact that the proper response was not forthcoming suggests two possible explanations. Either the authorities do not possess the necessary tools to influence economic and financial activities, which would imply that over the preceding decades the public had been deliberately misled about their capability to manage the economic situation. Or, alternatively, authorities have become increasingly and dangerously preoccupied with private interests at the expense of the public interest. Either case has implications of public morality, indicating the need for serious public discussion of the issue.

To end this section, I'd like to make one more remark that might seem somewhat irrelevant, but which deserves attention in light of the role moral attitudes and restraints played in macroeconomic performance during the crisis. As we have seen, the crisis in U.S. and European economies was driven primarily by the failure to resolve, in either the medium or the long term, the problem of significant "bad" debts and financial assets of dubious quality, so-called toxic assets. These issues, together with consumer demand drivers, constituted the main focus of the economic agenda in the United States when the new Obama administration took office, and they continue to make up the core topic of debate regarding the future of the world economy in the short and medium terms.

Moreover, most commentators and experts also believe that the long-term future of global capitalism will be dependent on the problem of outstanding debts, which have over the past few years reached unprecedented levels, both quantitatively and qualitatively. Many people—and I count myself among them—have come away with the impression that the scale of debt, primarily in comparison with the scale of activity in the real sector, has reached a level that puts at risk the sustainable development of the global economy.

Granted, the issues of indebtedness, its size and role, are largely technical. Problems associated with debt come not from its mere size but rather from its overall impact on demand and its structure, and the assessment of possibilities for its refinancing. Neither do I believe that indebtedness as such bears direct relation to morality—a view held by some conservatives. Moral hazard, strictly speaking, relates less to the actual size of debt amassed by an economy than to the failure of financial regulators to control the situation and the extensive opportunities for abuse of this system that follow. Even looking at the problem of debt from this angle, however, I find it difficult to ignore the correlation between its growing role and size on the one hand and the proliferation of irresponsible attitudes and practices on the other. Admittedly, this is a complex topic deserving separate detailed discussion.

Well-Known Causes

The chain of events culminating in the global slump has already been described in detail by those involved, and an outsider's view is unlikely to add much to the general picture. Moreover, dwelling on the triggers of the current financial troubles serves in part to distract the public from the underlying causes—complacency, self-deception, disregard for public interests, and in many cases open deceit and fraud on the part of both market players and regulators. Detailed debates are useful about who the victims are and how much they have lost, who deserves assistance, and the extent of this assistance. But finally the questions about what to do now obscure the fact that the recession was largely brought about by irresponsible actions or inaction on the part of those entrusted to keep the financial sector in order. Until we unflinchingly confront this fact, discussions of prescriptions for overcoming the crisis will lead nowhere.

The world economic crisis has been subject to numerous interpretations. A general consensus exists among most analysts, however, that the recession combines the impact of traditional cyclical factors and several specific phenomena in the financial sector in Western economies, primarily in the United States.

It is difficult to dispute this assessment if we limit ourselves to analysis of the immediate factors leading to the crisis, or if we make no attempt to understand the underlying causes or choose not to consider the crisis within a broader historical context. From a limited perspective, we could in theory focus solely on two sets of factors: 1) the regular emergence of various imbalances, including in prices, inherent in market economies, attributable to imperfections in the mechanisms governing interaction between supply and demand, valuation of resources and assets, and the like; and 2) various deviations engendered by the gap between activity in the financial sector and the state of the so-called real economy.

As for the first group of factors, the crisis has not yielded anything out of line with various developments over the past few decades. The cyclical nature of markets is attributable to imbalances related to the high degree of inertia in the signals emanating from consumers in the form of demand for a variety of assets and resources. This inertia, coupled with inevitable incidental distortions, disorients the supply of resources and introduces considerable distortions in the logic of market pricing.

In particular, the economy is inevitably subjected to asynchronous changes in end-user demand, which is volatile and difficult to predict, and interim demand, which determines movement of capital resulting in increased supply of different types of resources. End-user demand, in its turn, is distorted by fluctuations of prices of different types of resources, which are indicative of changes in interim demand and are essentially unrelated to actual supply costs. The unpredictability of demand for different assets to be used for investment purposes also introduces a significant element of uncertainty.

Usually incorrect price signals and resulting imbalances originate from factors intrinsic in a market economy, such as the lack of access to complete and reliable information, the spontaneity of variable psychology factors, the unpredictability of technological changes, and so on. Subsequently, however, these false signals are intensified by speculative short-term capital movements to those areas where rapid price growth for material and derived financial assets is expected. Faulty expectations lead to new misleading signals and accordingly to still more unrealistic price levels.

Inevitably, distortions and imbalances accumulate in the price system, resulting in misguided investment decisions and inefficient use of existing resources. When such imbalances grow large enough, the figurative "bubble" bursts: valuations of overpriced assets undergo a market correction, and an economic crisis is the result. As a rule, this leads simultaneously to the establishment of new price proportions and far-reaching redistribution of assets and resources among economic agents. Such a redistribution manifests itself most vividly in bankruptcies, mergers, and acquisitions, but is not confined solely to them. For example, the impairment of investment assets (especially investment-grade securities and real estate) and the rising value of monetary liquidity is (or at least used to be) a typical phenomenon during a crisis, which facilitates the redistribution of property from passive savers to active entrepreneurs.

In principle, fluctuations of this kind are natural, inevitable, and for the most part useful for the economy. Artificial obstacles to the correction of imbalances simply lead to their accumulation and a general reduction in efficiency before the inevitable (and, because postponed, more destructive) correction. From this perspective an anticyclical economic policy is useful, but it cuts both ways. The impact of such a policy on the economy and society can be considered positive to the extent that it irons out unavoidable fluctuations. However, if it begins interfering with timely price corrections and resource allocations, it may end up playing a pernicious role over the long term and may ultimately unhinge the economy.

Everything I have said so far applies to the 2007–2009 crisis. It is now recognized as a fundamental truth that a considerable number of bubbles, represented by vastly overvalued types of assets, accumulated in developed market economies and in the global economy toward the end of this decade. No one disputes that an incipient recession should make it possible to eliminate those bubbles temporarily, thereby lowering the market prices of corresponding assets in the medium term. In other words, the partial dependence of the recession on cyclical factors is obvious. Accordingly, the part of the crisis that leads to a correction in pricing ratios not only is harmless for the international economy, it is essential, merely evoking regret that the correction did not come sooner, when the imbalances to be eliminated were smaller and more manageable.

But the unprecedented vigor of the global economy for almost ten years before 2008 eased demand limitations, thereby allowing the prices of certain types of assets and resources to surge. As a result, the natural correction of these prices was bound to be accompanied by painful consequences. I am referring here not only to the financial sector, including excessive capitalization of banks and other financial institutions, but even more to the overheating that had been building up in some markets over years, including real estate in developed countries, and international markets for oil, metals, and other commodities.

Lax Government

The relative prosperity of the past decade had yet another consequence for the global economy that is inextricably related to the Great Recession. De facto the governments of developed countries, above all the United States, disregarded the principle that risk assumed by an individual economic agent is the sole responsibility of this agent, whereas the government, as represented by its regulatory agencies, shares risks communally assumed by a large number of agents. Here too, as with price growth, the interests of each economic agent induce it to take actions that would have an adverse impact on the interests of the market as a whole and each participant individually. Just as a single adjustment can lead to spiraling price hikes to the detriment of common interests, decisions by an individual player to raise risk levels in the drive for increasing profits can lead to the depletion of the safety margin of the system as a whole.[3] Similarly, just as the fight against inflation can be handled only by public regulators who rise above the interests of individual economic agents, the maintenance of the conditions required to ensure the stability of the financial (and more broadly, the economic) system can be discharged only by the state.

It is a natural function of a responsible government in a modern state to control the risks taken by private and publicly owned entities so that they do not reach the size where they may jeopardize functioning of the system at large; that function was disregarded in the past decade. Some governments neglected this duty overtly, others implicitly; in the end, however, all the responsible parties accepted the premise that the market was self-regulating and did not require state involvement or intervention with respect to the level of risks assumed by corporate players in the sectors where they operated. This assumption drove financial market deregulation, particularly in the United States. The Gramm-Leach-Bliley Act in 1999 was a milestone in the process. The act repealed the Glass-Steagall Act, which had established a legal distinction between investment and commercial banks back in the 1930s. Minimal regulation continued under the Bush administration, which took no action to prevent the granting of loans to dubious borrowers.[4]

The public rationale for self-regulation was that a mechanism would emerge spontaneously to mitigate various economic risks. But risks were not mitigated; they were merely transferred to newer and newer assets. In a number of cases, such as credit default swaps, it appeared at first that the risk had been distributed among a wider range of assets. In fact, the risks had been retained and even increased, assuming in the process latent and ambiguous forms and thereby provoking careless investments in financial assets. In general, risks grew in all areas of the economy.

Consequently, the inactivity of overconfident governments led to the transfer of risks in the private sector to the state through the purchase of toxic assets, the direct or indirect nationalization of credit institutions, the quasi-nationalization of shares of distressed industrial assets, and so on.

What's New?

As I have already suggested, the nature and causes of the Great Recession cannot be reduced to traditional cyclical factors or to distortions and problems within the financial sector. The downturn was to a large extent driven by or is closely linked to underlying problems in the behavior of economic agents in the market, from the disasters in the U.S. market for subprime mortgage loans and financial derivatives linked to these loans to the collapse of leading multinational investment banks and the de facto bankruptcy of the financial systems of a number of small European countries.

As these problems are not directly attributable to imperfections in the mechanisms that guarantee macroeconomic equilibrium, their influence should be treated as a completely separate cause (and aspect) of the crisis. Independently characterized by specific historical contexts and causes, these problems both overlapped with cyclical factors and provoked their manifestation in the volumes that we have been witnessing.

For example, the financial market meltdown, attributable to an abrupt impairment in the value of investment portfolios containing securities backed in some way by securitized mortgage loans, led investors and financiers to lose confidence in the stability of a significant number of financial institutions. This crystallized into a crisis of confidence and resulted in the tightening of loan conditions and reduction in the levels of borrowing on the interbanking market and on the nonfinancial sector. In turn, this credit freeze was the catalyst for the sharp deterioration in the financial position of many companies in the real sector, which had been adversely affected by the drop in consumer demand, primarily with respect to comparatively expensive goods for long-term use. At the same time, the threat of a serious recession in the developed part of the world resulted in speculation on the oil futures market. Investors who had previously bet on price rises and had in the process driven up the oil price, which almost tripled in one year, started aggressively offloading oil contracts. As a result, oil prices returned to mid-2007 levels within just a few months. The severe correction affected the prices of most other commodities, which also plummeted in the second half of 2008.

As a result, the global economy in 2008 was confronted by what amounted essentially to a standard set of problems: stringent demand limitations, decline in production, reduction in credit, and the formal or de facto bankruptcy of a number of leading companies that had been relied upon to prop up employment levels and earnings. In other words, the problems on the financial derivatives market, which had attracted the most attention for almost a year and had been considered the main and perhaps the only manifestation of the crisis, culminated in a more or less familiar standard economic recession.

Accordingly, public interest in these phenomena assumed the usual form: the public, including educated people, was less interested in the intricacies of a modern market economy and the reasons for the crisis than in receiving answers to the familiar questions: how to stimulate consumer demand; who would be allocated state funds and how much; what should be done about problems of crisis-stricken industries; and whether and to what extent it might be necessary to resort to protectionism to support a country's manufacturing base. In other words, almost every speaker on this topic started out from the assumption that the standard measures of anticyclical regulation—manipulation of interest rates, tax concessions, increasing state expenditure on infrastructure, and targeted use of state funds to alleviate the financial position of "socially important" enterprises—could be used to mitigate the impact of the recession and hasten its end. They also assumed that even if these measures turned out to be ineffective and impotent, the economy would in a year or two independently rectify the accumulated imbalances, eliminate distortions, and more or less automatically create the requisite conditions for a new period of dynamic growth.

Such assumptions seem to be widely shared by individuals of different position and spheres of activities—government officials, regulators, bankers, and analysts, for example—and there seem to be numerous arguments for it. But these arguments, which seem to omit very substantial phenomena beyond the familiar attributes of a conventional, cyclical recession inherent in a crisis, are fundamentally incorrect. To get an idea of such phenomena, I propose to try to look at it in a broader historical context.

Old Problems in a Historical Context

In reality the Great Recession of the early twenty-first century can be considered in two ways. On the one hand, as we have seen, all its components had already been observed in one form or other (and on more than one occasion), and this crisis has shown us nothing fundamentally new. On the other hand, we could look at it from a different angle: why have we seen no fundamental change in the way the modern economy works, or in its oversight by economic and financial authorities, over the past few decades? Throughout the twentieth century, in particular in its second half, significant technological and social advances have been brought to bear on the economy. Professionals in the field became increasingly knowledgeable and accumulated more skills, while the capabilities of state and public institutions increased. New institutions have been created over the past few years, assuming the role of financial market regulators, while improvements were introduced to the institutional and legal base for the functioning of markets.

Economic research after World War II outstripped prewar analysis by an order of magnitude, in both the number of publications and the coverage of topics. The body of data collected for this research and the available tools increased enormously. A powerful school of mathematical economics and econometrics emerged and aspired for a seat of honor among the exact sciences. The work of the economists of classical and institutional schools, who used reasoning to derive logical conclusions about economic phenomena in the broader context of laws of human society, was de facto reclassified within the fine arts. Economic science, in contrast, was accorded only one goal: the mathematical formalization of dependencies and correlations among economic variables, including an exact calculation of diverse economic risks.[5] Many felt—and still feel today—that the modern economy had become far more comprehensible than it had been in the middle of the twentieth century, and that its reaction to various changes in conditions or factors could be described in mathematical formulas and even calculated exactly up to three decimal places.

If we turn to matters of economic policy, every imaginable form of interdependence between macroeconomic indicators and parameters has seemingly been studied by the end of the last century. More has been written on the mechanism of "bubbles" than in the entire history of economic thought before the twentieth century. Tradition held that a dearth of information was one of the main causes of all manner of uncertainty and risk in a market economy, but in the past few decades the capabilities of modern society to gather and process information grew so much that they have surpassed the most audacious imagination.

New enhanced tools appeared on the market for hedging and insuring against risks. Market institutions offering such tools were, in turn, supervised by regulators to mitigate all types of commercial risks. Specialized agencies engaged in studying and tracing risks professionally, and market participants were presented continuously with new options to insure themselves against those risks. Investment banks and companies set up powerful analytical departments. Moreover, financial and major manufacturing and trade corporations set up in-house analytical departments to track macroeconomic trends and their impact on corresponding risks. Rating agencies diligently studied the creditworthiness of borrowers and securities issuers, hiring the best analysts on sky-bound salaries.[6]

Moreover, if you looked at business books in recent years, you found the message, implicit in some cases, explicit in others, that there would be no more crises of a comprehensive nature lasting for years. Your reading would have reflected a general conviction that today's financial authorities had learned how to defuse and avert acute imbalances and deviations from the accepted equilibrium and that new methods of collating and analyzing information had given the authorities an unprecedented ability to detect and control the most dangerous developments.

However, if this is the case, what went so disastrously wrong? Why were government regulators and businesses totally unprepared organizationally and psychologically for the outbreak of instability?

My answer to these questions, on which I shall elaborate in the subsequent sections, is that economic policy making and economic thinking that led to instability were dominated by vested interests, at the expense of public good and economic stability. In place of an honest and responsible approach, policy was based on false presumptions and a conscious disregard of inconvenient economic realities, and the self-interested manipulators of that policy were rewarded both individually and collectively by publicity and promotions, high salaries, and numerous perks, at the same time avoiding personal risks and responsibilities. This sort of policy making is the foundation of Realeconomik behavior.

Attempts to place individual blame for the troubles have not been serious. Compiling a list of several dozen famous people and declaring that they were solely responsible for the crisis makes sense only as journalistic license. Some people calling themselves economists claim that one or several wrong decisions—for example, a reduction in interest rates instead of an increase—may constitute the real cause for the worldwide vicissitudes, and even a breakdown of modern capitalism. However, such an explanation is too shallow to be true. The causes of such complex phenomena as the stock market crash, international crisis in the banking system, or global recession should be commensurate with the actual phenomena in both depth and scale.

Even if an individual human mistake could have such disastrous consequences, it should not be impossible, with the current intellectual and institutional capabilities, to create a mechanism of economic regulation that would be capable of detecting more or less automatically and rectifying incorrect decisions and thereby preventing them from disrupting global market stability or the international economy as a whole.

Unanswered Questions

So why on earth were the highly touted advances in economics science and the abilities of economic regulation unable to guarantee the immunity of the market economy to cyclical factors? Why did such progress leave the functioning of a number of fundamental institutions of the capitalist economy at risk? How did it happen that the quantity and quality of debts in the largest world economies were not sufficiently controlled by the supervisory controlling agencies? Why did "bombs" explode consecutively in various categories of securities backed by collateral that turned out to be inflated or blatantly inadequate? And why did this come as a surprise each time to those people, who theoretically could and should have noticed the increase in corresponding risks? Finally, why did the public and business, despite widely promoted anticrisis measures of governments and the reassurance of regulators, display their obvious distrust about the future by curtailing their operations?

Curiously, these questions are rarely posed. And if they are raised, they rarely receive a detailed answer. In the second half of the book I will detail my thoughts about why these questions are unpopular with professionals. But it should by now be clear that the answers to these questions are unlikely to be found within the realm of theory of economic policy. It would be the utmost naïveté to believe that the crisis was just a matter of inadequate data, wrong judgment, or a wrong book read before making a decision. Neither could it be attributed to misjudgments or even acts of corruption by particular decision makers. Any serious investigation of what happened to world financial markets in 2007–2009 must begin with the stipulation of a systemic failure related to the whole set of motives and limitations of the financial elites of the world's leading economies, as well as their public regulators and control bodies. I reject the notion that the crisis was born of policy mistakes committed by innocent officials devoted to ideals of social need and long-term stable development. At the heart of the problem is public negligence stemming from the decline of social responsibility and the resultant decreasing role of self-regulation mechanisms based on moral guidance. That decline requires priority attention.

The largely rhetorical questions I have posed can actually be viewed from a slightly different perspective. The whole of the past century was marked by two dangerous assertions that were unhesitatingly accepted by intellectuals: 1) the accumulation of knowledge creates vast opportunities to influence human society; and 2) humanity is following a specific path of progress, and the community of intellectuals knows that path.[7] Admittedly, the second assertion comes with an obvious proviso: the meaning of social progress has been subject to diverse interpretations, and much of the past century has been marked by intellectual, and at times armed, conflict. Still, the majority of leaders of public opinion, certainly in the developed part of the world, agreed that it was possible on the basis of mere intellectual effort to develop some optimal model for economic and political order and then use it to manage existing human communities. The defeat of the Soviet Union in the Cold War reinforced the beliefs of the mainstream political and economic elite in the West that it had already achieved the optimal model, which was by definition the only correct model.

It should be noted that the triumphant end of the Cold War for the United States had numerous political and economic consequences, not all of them positive, both for America and for the West. I will address them in due course. Here my salient point is that the increased belief of the Western elite that it had taken the right course played a considerable role establishing the prerequisites for the eventual crisis.

If we first try to understand why this overconfidence increased so perceptibly in the past few decades, we find other associated assumptions for this development.

Don't Worry, Be Happy

First of all, there were perfectly objective reasons, and to a certain extent even material grounds, for such confidence. The American economy had faced a number of potential cyclical crises in the 1980s, 1990s, and first decade of this century, but the authorities had managed to nip these in the bud with money from the Federal Reserve. Never mind that these interventions prevented the market from rectifying a number of imbalances that required regulation in the interest of long-term dynamic development. The American financial authorities appeared to have short-circuited these cyclical downswings. This apparent success created the belief that spontaneous economic fluctuations and market movements could to a large extent be controlled. In other words, the events appeared to support the claims that economic science was an exact science capable not only of explaining economic reality but of actively influencing developments.

Second, we have to take into account a principle of psychology encapsulated in the saying "If it ain't broke, don't fix it." If everything is going well, if the country and important individuals in the country are perceptibly growing richer over time, if your international competitors are buried under a variety of pressing problems while your own problems have if not disappeared at least become less acute—if that is the case, why bother looking for catches and hidden agendas and raising the alarm about risks that have yet to materialize and perhaps never will? This willful blindness affected both business, which willingly, if implicitly, delegated responsibility for the quality of management to governments, and politicians, who just as willingly assumed that if things were going well, there was no reason for them to suddenly turn bad. And the professional theoretical economists, riding the renaissance of trust in the free market as universal regulator, naturally took great satisfaction in reasoning that even the worst businessman or -woman instinctively knew better and was more efficient than any government, however competent it might be. These attitudes raised the level of general euphoria and created an environment that prevented advocates of administrative restrictions on market risks from gaining the support of influential proponents in government and business.

Third, psychological and social comfort encourages conformism and silent acquiescence in the general mood: the echo-chamber effect. This principle affects countless unknown "analysts," as well as people with a history of success in business, science, or policy making—people whose names inspired and continue to inspire awe when cited as the sources of published revelations.

From that perspective, it is quite telling that the same well-known and respected individuals, who until recently had not even hinted at the vulnerability of the economic model prevailing in the West for the fifteen to twenty years preceding the onset of the crisis, suddenly came full circle in early 2009 and started predicting the rapid and irrevocable collapse of the system. By way of illustration, we can refer to speeches given at a seminar at Columbia University in February 2009. After exaggerated assertions that "we [had] witnessed the collapse of the financial system," that "the world financial system has effectively disintegrated," the economic gurus unanimously condemned the entire precrisis model of capitalism, deftly termed "financial capitalism." The downturn, which had only one year earlier been depicted as a minor blip in the functioning of the banking sector that could be rectified with a comparatively small injection of liquidity without any need to tinker with the principles of self-regulation, was now increasingly characterized as "a turning point in the functioning of the market system."

A similar desire to fit in with mainstream opinion was, to all intents and purposes, a critical factor explaining the atmosphere of unwarranted optimism and complacency that was perceptible in the milieu of Western business and quasi-government elites throughout the 1990s and beyond.

Fourth, in addition to the purely psychological propensities of people not to contrive additional problems and concerns, a decrease in external pressures played a role. In the first forty years after the end of World War II, the threat of military confrontation with the Soviet Union and substantial military expenses related to this threat constituted an objective disciplinary factor, creating an atmosphere of inner tension in Western societies and prompting them to listen more attentively to critics, who highlighted failings and risks in government policies, including economic policy. It cannot be claimed that this was an extremely powerful factor—self-criticism often gave way to complacence and tolerance of abuses. However, the abrasive confrontation of the Cold War played a specific disciplinary and at times sobering role. If nothing else, it enabled the U.S. government to maintain control over financial markets whose health was deemed vital to national economic security.

Finally, several decades of plenty and peace brought forth a new generation that had never known deprivation and that was less inclined to question the rationale of the existing world order and more inclined to believe that the world was evolving in the right direction. The idea of "all-conquering universal progress" was implanted on the most propitious soil and yielded corresponding fruit. Many people had not simply avoided thinking about the issue: they sincerely believed that the underlying ideological questions of the contemporary world had been answered once and for all, and that convincing anyone who had not reached the right answers would be comparatively easy—or if not, could be achieved by force. A significant number of people simply stopped thinking about these issues, focusing instead on personal prosperity and adopting "postmodernist" indifference to public issues.

All these factors, taken together, engendered a powerful collective assurance about the rightness of the course taken by developed countries and about their ability to address economic problems within the scope of the existing paradigm of economic growth. This confidence in turn made it possible to overlook such worrying trends as the increased risks and tensions in the financial sector.

However, is that all there is to it? And what is behind such irresponsible collective overconfidence?

Rules of Behavior

Recent publications and speeches mention more and more frequently that the negative economic developments that built up over many years also have a specific moral context. Moreover, there are more and more interpretations of this issue.

At first, in autumn 2008, the moral assessment of the crisis was crude, unsophisticated, and thoroughly unscientific. Outrage was expressed about "greedy Wall Street bankers" and the "irresponsible actions" of hedge fund managers or mortgage institutions. Of course, everyone knows that greed, irresponsibility, and the tendency to take excessive risks with one's own and other people's money are eternal human vices, no more prevalent in human beings today than they were in Shakespeare's era or at the dawn of modern capitalism.

Moreover, human beings have by nature short memory spans, especially for events that are unpleasant and painful, or that evoke a sense of shame or uncertainty. But the claims that investment bankers and others involved in the crisis had lost all sense of decency were unfortunately as ineffective and their impact as short-lived as they were loudly proclaimed.

Eventually, however, the moral aspects of the events facilitating the crisis started to attract increasing and (more important) more reasoned and reasonable attention.

The persistent media emphasis on the moral aspect of the events leading to the crisis was marked by at least two key aspects. On the one hand, an increasing number of people believed that they could and should acknowledge its importance. If journalists were initially the only ones to refer to moral issues, a few months later, similar lines of reasoning began to appear in public statements by both American and European politicians.

This culminated in a number of statements by European political leaders, first and foremost Sarkozy and Merkel. The French and German leaders condemned the historical deadlock and "immorality" of what they now designated financial capitalism, which they contrasted with the "capitalism of production." In turn, newly elected U.S. President Barack Obama launched a systematic exposure of dubious practices—entrenched in the financial sector—from the perspective of moral values. Even in his inaugural address Obama noted that the weakness of the American economy was "a consequence of greed and irresponsibility on the part of some, but also our collective failure to make hard choices." What is particularly important about these words is that the accent is placed on collective attitude as well as on individual greed or mendacity. That is what I am trying to stress: that the challenges for an economy arise not from individual vices or weakness, which are natural and eternal, but from public attitudes and reactions which may channel individual behavior into completely different directions.

Finally, at some point high-ranking and authoritative economists stated that unsound moral standards had played an important role in the emergence and exacerbation of the crisis. Simultaneously (and this is key), there seemed to be a growing awareness, not only in bars and among the many newly unemployed, but also among the intellectual elite, the wealthy, and other politically influential people, that it is no longer enough to merely state that moral standards are low, but that we must also admit that this has been affecting the economy's performance. Many people feel more and more clearly now that there is an increasingly close link between, on the one hand, the ethical norms in public life and the consistency of their application and, on the other hand, the function of public institutions, including economic institutions.

Certainly much was written and said about the need for social institutions to maintain certain rules of behavior that go beyond legal norms and restrictions, to bring public reaction and moral persuasion to bear against vices like greed and lying. However, few observers perceived the direct link between the stability of moral norms in society and such specific phenomena as the movement of stock market indexes or the securitization of mortgage loans. None of the economic analysts in the period before the crisis predicted that constraints attributable to moral weakness could directly affect the short-term state of the economy.

If we return to the situation before autumn 2008, economists and regulatory agencies focused their attention on every kind of problem on the financial markets in the United States other than public morality and business ethics. These factors were assumed to be beyond the scope of economic analysis, and they were not in the line of vision of professionals who monitored developments, assessed commercial and political risks, issued recommendations on the necessary measures for regulating the markets, or carried out such regulation.

Even after it appeared that the local calamity on the mortgage bond market in the United States was either the cause or the trigger of the global slump, when the media seized on Wall Street greed and the fantastical bonuses for managers responsible for the dire straits of the companies they managed, even then the moral failure of senior government officials and senior management was not examined.[8] This moral failure still is not considered the essential cause of the widespread shocks to modern capitalism. A most authoritative report on the causes of the 2007–2009 financial crisis by the FCIC does mention "a systemic breakdown in accountability and ethics" as one of the factors that led to the crisis. Nevertheless, it sees it as a secondary factor that exacerbated the crisis rather than the prime reason explaining why it happened at all. Pointing out quite accurately the reluctance of those given the necessary powers to see the signs of the coming collapse and take necessary action to prevent the worst from happening, the report for the most part leaves open the question why they failed to act or preferred to stay supposedly ignorant of the danger signs. The question of ethics is in effect treated as a problem resting more with individuals entrusted by the society to play an important role in the nation's economic life than with the society at large, which is prepared to tolerate incompetence, negligence of duty, and outright deceit.

This is how I perceive the situation today, and I am not alone in this perception. I see it as symptomatic that the people who embody capitalism—and not just outcasts of the system—have begun to state that contemporary capitalism has approached a line beyond which further development on the basis of previous conceptions of society and management is impossible. If the weakness of moral principles in modern society is the underlying cause of the crisis (and I shall devote the rest of this work to substantiating this link to Realeconomik), then disagreements on immediate causes and possible repercussions of this particular recession—whether it lasts months or years—are secondary.

Perhaps by the time this book is published the recession will be widely seen to have come to an end, with the global banking system avoiding further turbulence thanks to anticrisis programs or irrespective of them. Even so, the principles or moral stewardship versus Realeconomik will contest our economic future.

In fact, in the fall of 2010, the National Bureau of Economic Research stated that the recession in the world's largest economy had ended in June 2009. But even then the NBER confirmed that, at least in terms of job losses, the recession was the deepest on record since the 1929–1933 Great Depression. More than eight million workers lost their jobs in the eighteen-month downturn that began in December 2007, surpassing the sixteen-month contractions of 1973–1975 and 1981–1982. The NBER did not conclude that the economy had returned to operating at normal capacity. Some economists predicted that it would not grow enough in the next several years to lower U.S. joblessness, which official figures put at near 10 percent (some unofficial estimates placed the jobless rate at closer to 18 percent). In addition, critics said, many corporations were taking advantage of near-zero interest rates to borrow cheaply and hoard cash while using stimulus funds to invest in technology rather than to hire workers on a large scale. Meanwhile, with the exception of some emerging market economies, sustainable growth prospects were dim from Japan to Europe.

Even when the world economic recovery becomes real and not just a figment of spin doctors' imagination, it will not signal the elimination of profound moral contradictions at the heart of the model of financial capitalism, contradictions that had a significant and perhaps dominant position in the global market economy by the start of this century. Consequently, the need to rehabilitate business and public policies rendered morally bankrupt by Realeconomik will be just as urgent.[9]

In subsequent chapters I will consider how moral factors were underestimated in economic life over the past few decades and try to suggest corrective mechanisms. However, first I will discuss the reasons why morality and economic activity should be perceived not as different dimensions of human society but as interdependent aspects of a single social organism. In particular, we must give serious attention to the link between, on the one hand, a specific level of compliance of business practice with certain fundamental ethical values and, on the other hand, the intensity and quality of economic growth, a link that has a more direct and immediate impact on the collective consciousness than is usually perceived.

2

Capitalism, the Market, and Morality

Trust

Few today would deny that a key role in the viability and efficiency of a market economy is played by the norms of behavior and values —including those we call morals—inherent in society, predetermined by mankind's biological makeup or socially conditioned. This influence is attributable primarily to the specific role of trust between economic agents in a market economy.

It has long been a given that agents' mutual trust, as well as the trust of each in government as arbiter and registrar, is essential to market relations both in theory and in practice. This trust has made possible the transition from the simplest market exchanges to complex economic relations involving economic agents separated by time and space. In capitalism today, trust continues to play a key role in financial and production activity and is reflected in such key economic indicators as the level of savings in general and bank deposits in particular, the propensity to invest in industrial and financial assets, the selection of forms of savings and investments, the scale of international capital flows, and so on.

Measures by state and public institutions to build public confidence in other economic agents stimulate investments, including foreign direct investments, and make it possible to maintain savings at a desired level or raise this level. Trust also increases the ability of regulatory agencies to adjust the rate and nature of the activities of economic agents, to influence their mood, to minimize or even eliminate the negative impact of certain external factors on the economy, and in general, to stimulate economic growth and introduce qualitative changes in the long term. If such trust is discovered to be unwarranted, however, the ability of economic policy makers and government institutions to address malfunctions in the economic system is undermined, regardless of their knowledge of economic rules, systems of control, and state-of-the-art regulatory systems.

Trust certainly doesn't exclude risks. Any economic action by individuals or business is affected by psychology, in the form of moods, expectations, and subjective assessments of market participants; thus uncertainty cannot be eliminated from the economic system, irrespective of the complexity and sophistication of the systems used by regulators to monitor and assess risk.

All economic agents, regardless of the information they have at their disposal, must assess how other market players will react to them and how they will behave as the situation changes. It might be assumed that individuals display a higher degree of rationality in their economic behavior than, for example, in political or cultural interaction. This would seem an even safer assumption in the case of economic professionals—their business behavior and reactions can be expected to be particularly rational. However, it is impossible to predict anyone's reactions perfectly, even in the presence of complete and accurate information, which is never the case in real life. That is why it is impossible to calculate the degree of risk attributable to a specific economic decision or action. It is wishful thinking to believe otherwise, and any work purporting to offer a formalized methodology for identifying close to risk-free business decisions is no more than intellectual gamesmanship.

In the final analysis, the adoption of a decision in business simply depends on whether an agent is willing to put at risk the resources at his disposal by entering into market relations and relying on specific actions by actual or potential counterparts in those relations. As the agent's experience and the experience of another party provide the only real benchmark, continued trust is an indispensable condition for the effective functioning of the market system.

From this perspective, only the ability to support or strengthen public confidence in economic policy makers and administrative institutions will determine the capitalist market economy's long-term future. Without this ability all efforts to solve individual problems or to attend to particular woes of business communities—tax burden, legal loopholes, inadequate infrastructure, excessive red tape, and so on—will be futile.

The possible consequences of losing this ability, dangerous locally, become disastrous in a global economy. Globalization, which I will cover in more detail later, multiplies the cost of miscalculations and errors, rapidly transforming local turbulence into global crises. Accordingly, an abrupt decline in confidence in several key economies introduces the risk of a global crisis for market institutions, with unpredictable consequences for capitalism.

Even the slightest change in economic agents' confidence in public and market institutions has a powerful impact on financial indicators. While in the "real" sector a 10 to 20 percent yearly change in output, prices, or investments is extraordinary, in the financial sector activity levels and prices often change by such multiples over the same period, because they are sensitive to the changing attitudes of investors. (To give an example, stock prices regularly change by the magnitude of tens of percentage points over a period of several months and even weeks, which could not be explained by changes in market conditions or situations within the firms. The only possible explanation lies in the impact of abrupt changes in expectations and confidence.) Accordingly, the greater the role of the financial sector in overall economic activity, the more radical is the potential reaction of the economy to such elusive items as change in the levels of confidence in economic institutions. Consequently, the greater the volatility of investment and consumer demand, the easier it is to trigger a deterioration in economic activity for no concrete reason.

Simple Rules of Effectiveness

Confidence, in turn, is linked not least (and perhaps even first and foremost) to the existence of public morality. Morality (rather than the legal dictates of the state) facilitates daily actions aimed at the production of goods, exchanges, savings, investments, and other basic economic actions. It provides the necessary degree of trust for millions of daily economic transactions to be conducted without an agent thinking each time of the necessity to guard himself against possible breach of contract or fraud by counterparties. In the absence of public morality, a large portion of today's business activities would be impossible because of prohibitive costs of securing enforcement of contracts.

Moral principles are so important in this process because state enforcement of compliance with the rules of market relations (in particular when implemented by so-called agencies of market self-regulation) is ineffective unless economic agents discharge them without duress; that is most likely to happen by virtue of adherence to principles of moral responsibility. If, say, nine economic agents out of ten stick to the rules not because of daily state coercion but because they consider it fair and rewarding, violations of these norms can be prevented or punished by authorized institutions in accordance with majority sentiment, with coercion applied only when strictly necessary. As a result, general compliance with the rules of the game set by society is achieved at a minimal cost.

For example, laws against theft, fraud, or bribery (to list just a few examples) work best when society at large considers those practices not just illegal but also immoral and unworthy of a responsible person.[1] If people known to be swindlers, bribe-takers, or organizers of fraudulent schemes are ostracized and boycotted whether or not they are prosecuted by law-enforcement bodies, enforcement of corresponding laws may be both effective and cost-efficient.

However, if a majority of agents in an economy are disinclined to comply with rules out of conviction or internal inclination to moral behavior, the costs of rule enforcement reach prohibitive levels and corresponding norms are simply disregarded. History has shown repeatedly that no laws can control corruption if the society sees no sin in trading administrative positions and the opportunities resulting from them. Legal action against tax evasion bears no fruit when it goes against public sentiment justifying tax fraud against governments considered illegitimate or inefficient. If discrimination against certain groups of people is deeply engraved in public moral attitudes, imposing effective laws against such discrimination incurs very high costs as long as these attitudes remain unchanged.

In other words, the state's ability to compel the public to obey the law is inherently limited for both economic and organizational reasons. These limitations may be more or less severe, but typically the government can achieve an acceptable level of compliance only with laws and rules perceived by most people as natural and just. If they are not so perceived by at least a significant proportion of the population, laws go unenforced and then become impractical. To ensure uncoerced majority compliance to rules, first, society must not tolerate amoral behavior, and second, the laws and rules of behavior, including business practice, should be consistent with socially accepted moral standards. Only then will the public develop the confidence in economic policy makers and political institutions required to support high savings rates, active investments in real and financial assets, and a minimal cost of lending.

I cannot offer data that would serve as a direct proof for these logical conclusions. But evidence is plentiful that Third World political regimes that have imposed by force laws not grounded in indigenous cultural and ethical practices accomplished little but alienation of the people, social unrest, mutinies, and even revolutions. Such conditions undermine economic growth, stable finance, and the climate for investment. And it is instructive that attempts by financial authorities in most post-Soviet economies to reduce the cost of finance failed in the wake of undisciplined business practices and rampant corruption justly associated with the decay of public morality in those countries.

In this respect, the concepts of morality and economic effectiveness, which at first appear to be totally unrelated, are in actual fact inextricably linked. According to a popular view, if the Protestant work ethic hadn't been ingrained in Western societies, promoting work, care, frugality in consumption, and honesty in dealings, there would have been no industrial revolution in the eighteenth and nineteenth centuries, and economic strength would have remained at the level of the Middle Ages. Conversely, the economic effectiveness of economic activity based on the norms of this morality promoted its preservation and to a large extent reinforced such behavior.[2]

Characterization of this ethic as "Protestant" should be understood as arbitrary. It would be incorrect to reduce ethics to the canons of any specific religious system. The set of values traditionally implied by this expression is shared, in varying degrees, by most religions. Similar values appear in the imperatives of various secular ideologies (quasi-religions). Moreover, the fundamental principles of societies in developed economies, in which public morality does not depend on religious consciousness, traditionally include such values as individual honesty, self-discipline, recognition of labor as the highest value, consideration of the collective and public interest, concern for other individuals, and the promotion of thrift and work for the good of future generations. It would be hard to find a single country among developed economies in which these values have been refuted publicly or the system of public morality has been built on fundamentally different values.

In fact, these values do not need to be substantiated by religion or philosophy, although both play important roles in the formation of public perceptions. Those who hold that moral values arose in human consciousness through biological evolution and competition between human communities are often no less zealous devotees of these values than are those who perceive them as divine instructions or esoteric knowledge.[3] Irrespective of the bases of these values, they are inevitably countered by psychological and behavioral influences we term vices, which unfailingly include, irrespective of the specific cultural background, falsehood, greed, hypocrisy, deceit, indolence, and an unbridled passion for consumption.

In my opinion the reasons for this are fairly evident. First, certain fundamental psychological traits serve as the basis for moral values without which humanity would never have stood out from the animal world after overcoming the resistance of the external environment.[4]

Second, and this is no less important, the modern developed world is the product of many centuries of competition, within which the presence of productive public morality constituted for a long time a trump card in the struggle of states and businesses for their place in the economic limelight. By contrast, the weakness or lack of sound moral principles led other countries or societies to be marginalized globally. The inevitable side effects: moral weakness, atomization of society, and the disintegration of communication constituted an impediment to economic and political progress, and thus to victory in international competition.[5]

In modern market capitalism, the effectiveness of moral principles in a society has a direct impact on the effectiveness of the economic system. Accordingly, attempts to preserve and increase effectiveness—within the scope either of a national economy or of the world economy—without focused efforts to support public morality and business ethics are bound to fail. If public morality falls and business ethics are eroded, then attempts to implement even the most valid ideas for encouraging the economy will prove abortive.

The same principle could be applied to politics as well, though the correlation between ethics and political effectiveness is less apparent and might be more visibly traced as a long-term trend. Admittedly, Machiavellian approaches historically have proved effective. But the history of the twentieth century has shown that solutions not guided by ethical principles tend to be short-lived and incur much greater costs in the long run. That was the case with the attempt to appease Nazi Germany at the outset of World War II, or, more recently, siding with antidemocratic regimes or forces as allies to fight the West's enemies in Afghanistan and in the Middle East: in the end long-term costs outweighed the benefits.

Anyhow, democratic political systems, whatever their shortcomings, have tended to outlive political regimes that ignored the issues of human rights, political and personal freedoms, rule of law, or social justice and stability.

In coming decades, ongoing globalization, which makes short-term partial deals utterly ineffective in the longer run, will certainly raise the efficiency of policies based on internationally accepted principles of respect for human rights, freedom of choice, equal and fair treatment of individuals, and social responsibility as necessary prerequisites of power and wealth.

Sources of the Financial and Economic Crisis

To apply my general observations about the influence of morality on economic effectiveness to the financial meltdown, I would like to return to some of the ideas raised in the first chapter. Let me recall the main doubt expressed in the previous chapter: neither the crisis nor the triggers—which contained, as we know, nothing mysterious or inexplicable—came as a shock that could explain the inability of the authorities to control the downturn in a timely way. The failure of the authorities and nongovernmental structures to react to the evident increase in risks and problems threatening the economy, which had been observed for a long time preceding the acute phase of the financial crisis, remains incomprehensible. It is this fact that leads me to think that the crisis has a very serious moral component—that is, that some factors behind it are related rather to a failure of public morality than to a shortage of data or of professionalism in those responsible for preventing imbalances and promoting stability. Moreover, easily identifiable ethical aspects, involving motives, goals, and restraining factors, played a part not only in the lack of adequate measures by economic agents and governments to prevent a serious breakdown but in the way the crisis gradually unfolded.

This moral aspect is not incompatible with other dimensions of the crisis, above all the need to correct structural and price imbalances and problems with regulation in the financial sector. However, it provides a perspective from which we can see this crisis as a consequence of a fundamental slackening of the value system, inherent in modern capitalist society, leading to a slackening of control by the authorities and self-regulating segments of the economy. In other words, the financial crunch and consequent systemic difficulties are not attributable to specific mistakes by specific individuals—see the notorious list of the twenty-five "authors" of the financial crisis compiled by journalists[6]—but instead represent a general letdown in the determination and ability of financial regulators to take effective measures to avert or mitigate economic shocks.

This lapse is a moral, not an economic, phenomenon and is related to changes in the moral climate in society. Realeconomik, manifested in a willingness to operate outside the framework of the rigid norms of ethical capitalism, created a situation in which unwarranted growth in risks to the stability of the financial sector, both national and international, failed to arouse an adequate response on the part of financial authorities.

Intellectual Honesty

However, before I address the general trend of the regression in recent decades in ethical constraints in business that encouraged the evolution of the crisis, I should like to highlight some other phenomena of the same nature that are more specific and closer in time.

If we look closely at the financial events of 2007–2009, something related to morality rather than economics becomes apparent at the outbreak of each stage. Even if the moral aspect of the problem appears immaterial at first glance, a closer look unfailingly leads to the conclusion that in the final analysis the actual outbreak and intensification of the problem are related to disregard for moral norms and tolerance for the blatant violation of such norms. This tolerance is a principal attribute of Realeconomik.

For example, what gave rise to the U.S. mortgage securitization debacle? First and foremost, it was caused by the irresponsible attitude of banks that initially granted unsound mortgage loans and then sold to other credit institutions securities (mortgages bundled into bonds) backed by payments owed on these loans (de facto expected nonpayments). They also created other "toxic" financial products based on securities that they knew to be unreliable, selling and reselling them along a chain to new credit institutions or institutional investors. The risks on these financial shares were insured and reinsured many times over. Furthermore, the financial institutions that acted as insurers (via credit default swaps, collateralized debt obligations, or other mechanisms for assuming risks on unreliable securities) closed their eyes to the extremely high risks of default. Finally, the institutions that had invested money—entrusted to them by individuals with the consent of paid advisers—in opaque and obviously risky financial products violated written and unwritten norms of conscientious behavior in financial business.

This happened because a percentage commission was paid at every level —to brokers, mortgage loan originators and servicers, financial institution officers, bank division consultants, structured finance units at ratings agencies, their lawyers and senior corporate executives, bank investment advisers, and so on—for arranging the loans, insuring, reinsuring, securitizing, and resecuritizing them. The long-range outcome—repayment of the loan— was of no interest to anyone in this chain. They were interested only in the process, the fees, and the accompanying profit. When interest rates rose and homeowners could no longer afford monthly mortgage payments and defaulted on the loans, the servicers—companies that collect payments on behalf of the investors who purchased the bonds made up of bundled mortgages—started foreclosing on the loans.

The U.S. mortgage debacle was compounded in late 2010 when Bank of America, the nation's largest bank, temporarily suspended foreclosures in all fifty states because of flawed paperwork and sloppy procedures hastily adopted by lenders in the subprime feeding frenzy. Other institutions joined the moratorium on foreclosures, further inflaming the still depressed U.S. housing market and threatening to precipitate another financial crisis.

Details of what Wall Street participants knew about the toxic financial products sold to investors and, when they knew it, were being made public in regulatory actions and private lawsuits. In the United States, hearings held by the Financial Crisis Inquiry Commission (FCIC) revealed voluminous evidence of widespread nefarious practices on Wall Street. The run-up to the crisis involved a grand fraud involving tens of thousands of people, if not hundreds of thousands—from ordinary brokers to the senior executives of major financial institutions, each of whom received a small or not-so-small interest and therefore at best did not object to the buildup of increasing risks in the financial system. Each person incurred a share of professional and moral costs proportionate to the amount of money over which he or she could take decisions.

The risks—both existing and potential—assumed by the big banks and home loan lenders also increased, in part because these lenders created and sold new investment products without taking the time adequately to assess associated risks and notify their clients about these risks. Such operations involved de facto collusion between these financial firms and the management of rating agencies, because the large-scale peddling of countless dubious products—for example, triple-A tranches (or bond classes) of mortgage-backed securities, triple-A tranches of asset-backed securities or securities backed by home equity loans—simply couldn't have happened without the investment-grade ratings. The ratings agencies' structured finance analysts, managers, and lawyers accorded the speculative securities of the investment firms those exceptionally high ratings—triple A and A1—thereby setting up their clients. Naturally, today these agencies deny that they intentionally sought to deceive investors and can even turn for support to such authoritative advocates as former chairman of the Federal Reserve Alan Greenspan, who asserted that the agencies "did not know what they were doing."[7] However, one must be naïve to believe that the ratings of the investment banks were unrelated to the huge fees they paid the ratings agencies. This is similar to the claim that contracts for tens of millions of dollars linking Arthur Andersen auditors with Enron in no way influenced the propensity of the auditors to close their eyes to the numerous skeletons in Enron's closets.

But the chain of participants does not end with the rating agencies. Credit, insurance, and other financial institutions are today overseen by different types of regulators, whose functions include control over the financial risks assumed by all these institutions. As a rule, institutional investors have collective management bodies as well as all types of supervisory boards or oversight committees. The financial regulators, as well as oversight and other such bodies, employ sufficiently skilled people who knew full well about the problems that could arise from the irresponsible behavior of the people they were regulating, but who chose for different reasons to close their eyes. This could have been attributable in part to the empty-headed misconception that the use of mechanisms for spreading risk (insurance, hedging) would somehow reduce the aggregate risk. However, the fact that this argument was preemptively presented as indisputable suggests that those involved well understood that spreading the risk cannot prevent consequences from materializing. For the most part, however, an adequate explanation of irresponsible behavior would be nothing but trade in conscience by those authorized to maintain strict and dispassionate supervision over the work of their subordinates with various financial instruments and assets.[8]

Regulation of the financial services sector underwent several waves of liberalization in the 1980s and 1990s, in particular in the United States. As well as relaxing constraints that had been introduced to protect clients from excessive speculative actions by managers of financial institutions—specifically investments not backed by sufficient collateral—the management systems at these institutions, remuneration systems, and dividend policies were freed from any controls.

Obviously, the short-term implications of removing these restrictions were understood by those who lobbied for deregulation and by implementers and advocates for such liberalization. They leveraged for this purpose their own authority and the authority of others, including representatives from business and interested parties in research institutions who were ready to substantiate the possibility of effective self-regulation in financial markets. The same people now justify their behavior by claiming that a major crash had not been predicted by mathematical models, and that they had sincerely believed that the financial system would "digest" any problems. This claim is believable only if it comes from armchair theoretical scholars and fanatical believers in the "invisible hand."

Instead, these statements come from professional practitioners working in the financial markets—or they reflect the position of Greenspan, who was categorically opposed to the regulation of the over-the-counter market in financial derivatives and hedge funds, maintaining that they helped to transfer risks from the bank system to numerous market participants and that this rendered the system far more stable.[9] Today those assertions are hard to take seriously.

The deregulation of financial markets cannot be attributed to commonplace corruption, although this also played some role. The motive of psychological comfort and indirect profit was more influential: it is always more pleasant and useful to maintain and increase wealth by going with the general flow, instead of resisting it or pointing out the errors and dangers of steps supported by influential interest groups.

While personal gain may not have been the overriding goal for most of the people orchestrating the removal of constraints, the process was made possible by an overt relaxation of internal checks best characterized as moral.

Any assumptions about the motives underlying the actions taken by people able to influence the course of events would be mostly guesswork. No evidence can be produced to prove that self-interest or neglect of duty inspired dubious decisions; other possible causes include the momentum of previous experience, lack of information, or sincere belief in the rightness of decisions that had been taken. And it is quite natural that people responsible for those decisions now defend their stance and the line that they took at the time as earnest and well founded.[10]

However, I find it difficult to accept these explanations. The degree of complacency displayed by regulators in the years preceding the crisis suggested that public attitudes toward their activities had become too lax, reflecting at least in part a general moral laxity in the society characteristic of a post–Cold War relaxation of self-discipline in the West.

Most of the decision makers in the processes that culminated in the crisis understood as specialists that what was being done was dubious, on both a professional and personal plane, but assumed that matters would work out in the end. "After all, everyone was doing it." "We'll fix it later." And besides, the personal revenue stream was very persuasive. Whether in most cases these participants were being honest or dishonest with themselves remains for them to answer.[11]

Different Ethics for the Uppermost Caste

However, the dubious transactions conducted by top management of credit and investment institutions, and the fact that the financial authorities closed their eyes to the development of the crisis, reflect only half the problem. In the course of the crisis another circumstance emerged: moral relativism became a factor in the decision making of the majority of company leaders in the so-called real sector of the economy. Everybody knows that the crazy amounts spent on external appearances by senior executives of companies in desperate financial straits (such as the $1.2 million in office refurbishments by the former Merrill Lynch CEO) represent the tip of the iceberg. The official expense accounts of top management of the U.S. automotive companies that appealed to the federal government for bailouts contain purchases of luxury bathroom fixtures and other such extravagances.

Management compensation deserves special attention. More and more scandalous stories are coming to light about the huge bonuses received by managers of investment banks, companies, and funds at a time when those structures had started recording losses that were the direct result of the investment strategies elaborated and implemented by those very managers.

As for senior managers who received big bonuses in times of crisis, one could not possibly blame them personally. They may sincerely believe they deserved the compensations stipulated by their contracts, whatever the situation was. After all, they are not owners of their firms but hired managers who don't have to cut their expenses out of sympathy for their employers.

Something else is telling: many people knew about these unwarranted bonuses. However, none of them informed those who could have prevented what in essence constituted the misappropriation for personal gain of other people's money. Alternatively, the people capable of bringing an end to this shameful practice for some reason chose to do nothing. This in turn suggests that a certain corporate ethic—the sense of an appurtenance to a privileged corps of highly paid managers—has taken root among top management professionals. This ethic establishes specific rules of behavior that apply only to the people in the inner circle, while everyone else is perceived to be of some other grade, subject to different moral standards, people existing primarily as fodder expected to generate income for the elite.

I am not talking here about schemers such as Bernard Madoff, who with the support of his clients consciously pitted himself against society and the law.[12] I am talking about people who sincerely believe that they are the cream of society, its best and brightest representatives. These people do not set themselves against the law; on the contrary, they willingly leverage protection of the law and do all they can to make sure that legislation effectively protects their interests from the claims and complaints of clients and shareholders. Moreover, they do not shun publicity, readily presenting themselves as the "enlightened," with unique knowledge and experience entitling them to demand special treatment and a commensurate level of compensation.

However, the following issue is even more interesting: none of the people whose unbecoming behavior during the crisis became known to the public feared exposure and public condemnation. In essence, no condemnation followed even after the scandalous reports about them in the media. There is a serious problem with the moral attitude of society if that society has become tolerant of frauds and crooks who perceive the threat of social isolation as nothing more than empty words.[13]

3

Shifts in the Global Economy of the 1980s–2010 and Changes in the Moral and Psychological Climate

Structural Shift: From Industrial Capitalism to Financial Capitalism

It's time to return to the overall picture. The examples I have cited reflect individual events and therefore cannot reveal the catastrophic phenomena underlying the recent financial crisis. The most significant and simultaneously most dangerous aspect of the crisis is attributable to the fundamental structural shifts directly related to a gradual slackening of moral constraints in developed countries. These structural realignments are cited with increasing frequency in economic literature in connection with the crisis and even more so with concerns that the global economy could be subjected to far greater disruptions than a brief slowdown in growth or contraction in GDP for several quarters. These fundamental shifts are increasingly viewed with special attention and sometimes with apprehension. The most prominent of them is a realignment from an industrial economy to a "postindustrial" or "new" economy. Structural shifts like these follow very fast growth of the financial sector and services directly related to it, as opposed to the traditional industrial sector; a growing intellectual rights component (or compensation of research and development expenses) in total cost of products; and the concentration of intellectual rights (and hence incomes attributable to them) in the hands of a few super-large corporations based mainly in the developed countries.

I wrote extensively about the latter in a book published in Russian several years ago.[1] There I examined fears that new and deeply entrenched divisions were being built between owners of intellectual rights and other economic agents both within and between national economies—divisions that in the long term would be detrimental to the efficiency and dynamism of business activities. I also looked at the growing dependence of modern Western economies on intellectual innovations. Contained within this dependence is the possibility of increasing manipulation of consumer behavior by those holding control over these innovations in order to secure privileged positions, effectively eliminating or limiting competition in large sectors of the economy. Furthermore, the ability to manipulate consumer behavior can lead to reduced transparency in matters of costs and utility of products, weakening public control over business and leaving more leeway for misconduct in matters of public importance.

Several years ago such fears were voiced rarely; most writers who voiced them, myself included, were considered outsiders. This was indicative of the period: an atmosphere of self-assurance, combined with general confidence that the West had taken the right path, easily overcame any skepticism, and such writers were portrayed as village idiots warning of the end of the world on a bright sunny day.[2]

Having witnessed the recent acute turbulence in the financial sector, some market participants are apprehensive that there may be still more disturbances to come, and that puts the abovementioned shifts in a somewhat different light. At first glance the Great Recession may not appear to be connected to those structural shifts, but that is at first glance only. Moreover, investigating the correlation between crisis and long-term shifts in the world economy brings to mind the fact that structural changes, on which I will dwell in this chapter, bear a clear impact on public morality, which in its turn played a role in bringing about an economic meltdown.

The first and perhaps key issue to highlight against the backdrop of the crisis concerns the change in the nature of the economies of developed countries that will soon be irreversible. The main thrust of this change is an increasing role of the tertiary sector, which embodies all kinds of services, both private and public, but primarily corporate business services. This change is attributable primarily to the unavoidable increase in the cost of certain resources in developed countries, especially the cost of simple labor and land. The need to cut these costs—pragmatism is, of course, a key aspect of Realeconomik—dictates the transfer of resource-intensive economic activities to less developed economies that have such resources in plentiful supply. The transformation of China and the countries of Southeast Asia into "the world's factory" is already a *fait accompli*, and further changes can be expected to bring India and some Latin American countries into the global industrial zone. In other words, the departure of mass production of goods from the developed world to "new industrial economies" over the past twenty years has become one of the main vehicles of change in the global economy, its structure, and the logic of its evolution.

What remains in the developed countries? Theoretically, industries based on high technology and/or focused on services that are either geographically specific or based on an exclusive intellectual, administrative, or political resource. (The indispensable presence in every developed economy of a standard-size trade and service sector for its population and the basic needs of local business is a given.) This is the theory arising from active international trade and the decisive role of comparative advantages.

But the actual picture is different from the theoretical conclusions. As we shall see, the structure of developed Western economies is increasingly characterized by the prevalence of sectors and activities based on manipulating consumers' psychology and preferences rather than catering to their intrinsic wants and needs, or to the needs of development.

This manipulation is possible because of two factors vital to the Realeconomik environment: power economics and amorality. First comes the dominating position of developed countries in the international economy and politics, which allows them to impose on the world specific patterns and standards of consumption and business practices. Then follows a general weakness of public morality and ethical restraint, which allows manipulative and socially detrimental businesses to proliferate and influence society and government decisions.

High Advertising Technologies

Theoretically, the specialization and structure of the different parts of the world economy could be expected to develop and progress along the lines set by the rationale of comparative advantages, constantly modified by international migration of such core economic resources as labor, capital, and intellectual resources (technologies and intellectual rights). On the surface, distribution of roles in the world economy between national economies and groups of countries seems to roughly correspond to this logic. However, a closer examination leads to a number of important qualifications.

The first qualification relates to the conventional wisdom that the most developed economies increasingly depend on the high-tech sector as the largest and perhaps the main source for their growth and development. In fact, the "high technologies" loudly and proudly advertised by transnational corporations are to a large extent hypothetical. There are indeed among them some technologies presupposing a significant intellectual component and a large degree of innovation. At the same time, however, the activity based on them cannot, even theoretically, generate employment or income of a magnitude sufficient to support a significant portion of the population of any large country. The role of high technologies as the backbone of the economy in Europe or the United States is no more than a myth that represents certain aspects of reality, misrepresenting reality per se.

Moreover, such symbols of technological progress in the private sector as new generations of mobile phone technologies (3G, 4G, and others that will follow), global positioning systems (GPS), and so on are the direct result of achievements that were made decades ago and have been extensively used in areas under strict government control—that is, in military and space technologies and the like. The introduction of these technologies into business projects is simply commercial use of once-secret military technologies or microwave frequencies that had been reserved for military use, for example, rather than fresh technological development. The standard set of subsequent implementation includes an early start of production in China, brand building, and marketing.

Most references to a high-tech economy actually describe activity that relies on the technological component for advertising and branding a product. What technical driver might there be in the development of a new formula for lipstick or shampoo, or one of ten thousands of different branded food products, or just as many kinds of household appliances and electronics, communications devices, household products, office supplies, and so on? Nevertheless, companies from developed countries operating in different sectors constantly position themselves as high-tech companies that supposedly perform active research and development and regularly achieve innovative results. But even if a product's technical attributes or

consumer value do not significantly change, the façade of "high-tech status" has become an indispensable aspect of corporate business strategy at
a time when the constant upgrades of products and regular launches of
"new" products on the market are recognized as a company's decisive
marketing and competitive advantage. (Experts maintain that substantial
product upgrades appear in most industries only once a decade.) Mobile
phone companies working in a competitive environment constitute a good
example. Serious technical solutions that result in offering their clients
really new possibilities of considerable value are rare and occur once in
several years at most. But the need of each company to position itself as
innovative prods it into introducing and advertising new services or possibilities every several months, producing an illusion for the consumer that
a product purchased a year ago is obsolete.

Another good example is the growing industry of health-related products that lure consumers with aggressive advertising of still more "innovative" technologies and products allegedly resulting from profound and
costly R&D activities, rarely, if ever, substantiated with verifiable evidence.

So when experts talk about the growing role of high-tech production
in the modern economy in the West, we should remember that a large part
of these high technologies is only remotely related to technological progress per se. In many cases, "innovations" presented to consumers as nearly
revolutionary are no more than mere repackagings of existing technical
solutions.

A second important qualification relates to the high number of international business services established in the economies of developed countries. This circumstance is attributable to historical tradition and has less to
do with the competitiveness of the providers of these services than with a
sort of historical rent they can include in their costs.

It is theoretically possible for almost any developing country to spend
enough cash to create a financial-services center that could match London,
Zurich, or New York in technical prowess and infrastructure. To compete
with traditional financial centers in the Western world, however, a developing country would have to overcome a dearth of historical tradition, and
tradition cannot be created quickly at any cost. The more than $2 trillion
of foreigners' money held in Swiss banks is the product of centuries of history, which cannot be arbitrarily modeled and reproduced in other conditions. It is just as impossible to model and reproduce London's City, or

Amsterdam's stock exchanges, in a different place, even if the new place is accorded preferential tax breaks or necessary modern facilities.

It is just as difficult to create from scratch a research and development center in a remote place far from the Western centers, even if one is prepared to pour in billions of dollars. That is why no special science or technology innovation "special economic zones" can ever create an effective serious alternative to Silicon Valley or the nuclear research center in Los Alamos.

A third qualification relates to the sustainable gap in living standards, in addition to the differences in cultural traditions, that provide a unique opportunity for developed countries to skim the cream of human potential from the rest of the world, attracting and retaining the best intellectual and organizational resources. For people employed in sectors producing intellectual products of considerable value, money is not all that matters. The sense of belonging to a professional circle associated with the renowned and prestigious American or European centers, as well as safe, secure, and comfortable living conditions not easily attainable elsewhere, often is of more importance for these people than high pay and easy promotion to administrative positions. The gap in living standards also guarantees the West the ability to attract a young labor force to work in servicing sectors.

Postindustrial Services

The most important aspect relating to recent structural shifts in world economy, however, is of a somewhat different nature and concerns the content of services that increasingly form the shell of Western economies.

Over the past few decades developed countries have aggressively leveraged their potential in various ways to replace the industrial economy with a postindustrial one. They gradually rejected expansion and retention of the processing industry and opted instead for management, planning, research, and innovation at the headquarters of transnational business empires and for providing a growing number of increasingly sophisticated financial brokerage services. Industrial capitalism in this part of the world is being rapidly replaced by financial and broker capitalism.

In principle, this process is neutral in terms of cost effectiveness: it can lead to either an increase or a contraction in efficiency. In cases where brokerage (including financial brokerage) facilitates cost optimization, it is a welcome process, which can represent a solid basis for the development of entire nations. At the same time, the promotion of such services can become an end in itself, thereby creating a distinctive pyramid in which the availability of financial or intermediary services generates subsequent demand, whether genuine or artificial, for other similar services. Additionally, the ability to build more complex integrated services promotes irrational bloated expansion of this sector, thereby leading to the long-term inflation of a bubble and a decrease in the sustainability of the economic system as a whole.

Financial services per se constitute one example of what I have in mind. Rightly justified in terms of achieving greater cost effectiveness, the functions of cash management and lending accrue related services, such as the insurance of financial transactions, consultation on investments and fund management, and the structuring of complex financial products for financial institutions and intermediaries. All manner of analysts elaborate more and more original schemes for investments and simultaneously offer supporting services.

The risks that are insured and then reinsured become less comprehensible and more opaque and require (at least in theory) more sophisticated and formalized analytical and valuation methods. Specialist firms are brought in for this purpose, such as rating agencies, which are in turn compelled to substantiate in some way their assessments and conclusions, creating demand for people capable of elaborating from existing material (often meager and unreliable) supporting data for various (mostly predetermined) conclusions that appear substantial. All of these firms also generate demand for mathematicians and programmers, who would supply them with the necessary formalized software and tools to process the data.

At the same time, these firms need to have at hand sufficient material that describes developments in the economy by function and industry, thereby creating specific demand for intellectual products, few if any of which the economy had previously required.

Subsequently the financial markets increase in size, and the number of people working there, as well as in adjacent industries, also increases. These people, mostly ambitious individuals inclined to self-promotion and to the projection of an aura of importance and mystery around their activities, induce demand for services designed to attract more money to this sector. Naturally they also create demand for related financial analysis, which attracts a sizable number of intellectuals working in the media.

The media outlets specializing in market information and analysis constitute an example of services growing out of the self-perpetuating expansion of financial markets. Contrary to popular belief that their reporting is meant for professional market players, their audience in fact mainly consists of people who have little professional relation to financial markets but are actual or potential clients of investment brokers and consultants. A large part of business news and analysis, which is regarded by the general public as part of the art (or magic) of financial activity, is in effect nothing but slightly veiled advertising aimed at attracting more clients' money into the financial sector. Nevertheless, it produces material demand for professional writers with expertise in this field, as well as for those who gather, process, and supply these writers with information.

All these people cannot appear from nowhere—they have to be educated and trained—and that creates demand for educational services and business training with the requisite flexibility. In turn, numerous intermediaries and consultants join in. As a result, the number of people connected to this sector either directly or indirectly increases faster than the sector of actual financial services.

A similar mechanism functions in many other areas, generating a vast multitiered network of frequently reciprocal services, which constitutes the shell of the postindustrial economy. The system is starting to function to a large extent for its own needs, involving more and more new people in its orbit, while the connection between their activity and initial requirements arising from the real needs of business optimization in other sectors is ever less perceptible, until it is completely lost. "Postindustrialism" gradually assumes a distinctive form of economic postmodernism, in which all meaning evaporates and momentum grows for economic structures to live their own lives, become self-fulfilling prophecies, and beget a whole series of newer structures that are in no way connected to the original goal of producing obviously new value.

This "new economy," which we would expect by definition to be extremely flexible by virtue of its low threshold of fixed investment and because it needs no expensive special equipment, is in fact no more elastic than its industrial counterpart. If demand falls and the foundation of the pyramid of services contracts, the remaining segments do their utmost to avoid reductions and retain their place in the system, partly by replacing the real demand for services with an ersatz demand that they try to create through inflation of their own significance and prospects. People who have accessed this "new economy" and found a niche there are reluctant to leave and appear ready to make significant sacrifices to retain the style of life to which they have become accustomed.

A financial broker, for example, would not quit his profession once he finds demand for his services shrinking. Rather, he would be inclined to compensate for his falling income from financial brokerage by selling his professional expertise as a lecturer at educational establishments, as an expert working for mass media, or as a consultant at some institution related to financial services. Quite naturally, in his new occupation he would do the best he can to convince outsiders that the art of making money by means of investment in financial assets and products represents one of the greatest achievements of human intellect, one that should be viewed with awe, envy, and respect.

This also holds true for the so-called high-tech component of the post-industrial economy, which allows companies through the promotion of actual or purported innovations of products that they launch on the market on a regular basis—associated with allegedly significant R&D expenses—to retain high margins on the end product, creating profits out of thin air.

What makes the process possible, aside from nontransparency of the cost calculations, is the inability of the consumer to assess the real value of innovations before or even after purchasing a new product. One reason is that objective assessment of the product's enhanced (or allegedly enhanced) qualities either requires prolonged tests or is impossible without specialized laboratory equipment.

Another reason lies in the fact (stated by Herbert Marcuse as early as the 1960s) that mass-consumption society, in which advertising prevails over individual judgment, makes it virtually impossible for an individual to distinguish his real needs from false ones.[3]

This is also attributable to the second major structural shift to affect developed countries during the decade or two directly preceding the crisis —a virtualization of a "new economy" that can exist and even develop over a protracted period of time in isolation from what is sometimes termed, perhaps inappropriately, the "real sector"—the production of goods and services that directly satisfy consumer and investment demand or are subject to intermediate consumption.

Virtualization of the Economy

The virtual nature of the "new economy," toward which the more developed economies have been moving at a growing rate over the past two decades, is marked by the deemphasis on basic production resources, such as labor, capital, and land. Unlike industries of the primary and secondary sectors—agriculture, mining, and manufacturing—in which products are visible and palpable and economic activity is inseparable from extraction or physical processing of resources, economic activity in modern business services industries is for the most part reduced to the redistribution of revenues and rights unrelated to the distribution and use of physical resources.

Much trading in financial products, for example, is, essentially, gambling for cash: the participants in the process play by rules that they have to a large extent drawn up themselves, trading "moves" in the form of various orders or products of intellectual invention. By devising ever more complex "packaging" of existing financial assets and their derivatives, professional players in securities and other related markets manage to redistribute incomes and assets without leaving their (increasingly virtual) offices and coming in contact with physical reality. Advances in electronic technology, which eliminated the need to vest the "moves" of market players with paper or provide any other material form, have made the virtual nature of this activity even more obvious.

The heightened influence of the financial sector and related services has undermined the concept of productivity and efficiency in a developed country's economy, because traditional economic calculations have little practical meaning.

This has been overtly demonstrated by the recent financial crisis: all discussions by economists of trends regarding the use and productivity of fundamental economic resources, based on analysis of the situation in the "real sector" of the economy, turned out to be useless in guiding practical action for economic policy. For example, measures aimed at influencing the use and productivity of economic resources in the nonfinancial sector—such as tax incentives for certain business activities or carefully designed and placed public investment programs—have virtually no impact on the actions of credit institutions, investors, and consumers in the financial sector, which seem to follow their own rules. At the same time, these actions have an enormous impact on the state of the market and the mood of participants in the most varied markets, triggering shifts of epidemic proportions in purchasing power and control over assets between individual economic agents and entire population strata.

In other words, a significant (and growing) proportion of general economic activity is becoming "virtualized." Even more important, the "virtual" aspects of the economy are increasingly influencing activity that could be arbitrarily classified as part of the "real" economy. Consequently, even a temporary increase in uncertainty in financial markets may destabilize the investment process enough to make protracted industrial decline possible and even inevitable. Falling prices for financial assets, even for reasons far removed from the economic sector, affect the moods and consumer behavior of vast numbers of people. Consumer behavior in turn becomes an insurmountable force capable of undermining production or inflating yet another economic "bubble."

The disassociation of a growing part of economic activity, in particular in the financial sector, from its original base, the productive use of fixed assets, has had another intriguing consequence: a general decay in the transparency of financial flows—movements of financial resources both within large business groups and between them, nationally and internationally. This may at first glance appear paradoxical. But recent events graphically demonstrated that despite claims that big business has been fighting for transparency, governments know even less about the real financial situation and financial flows at major companies than was the case, for example, forty or fifty years ago. This holds particularly true for companies in the financial sector, where rapid growth in the size of the sector in recent decades, combined with complicated relations within the sector and growth in management's technical ability to implement vast numbers of complex transactions over extremely short timelines, has eroded transparency.

This was also demonstrated by an absolute and relative increase in the amount of money taken out and exported to offshore jurisdictions. If the numbers appearing in the media are to be believed, the amount moved to "special" jurisdictions exceeds $10 trillion, although it is in fact impossible to trace all the money flowing out. How can you follow money invested, for example, in an American fund that has subsidiaries in the Cayman Islands, through a Panamanian company that must be contacted through a consulting agency registered in Liechtenstein?

The use of offshore tax havens long ago became a widespread and virtually mundane phenomenon in the United States and Europe. According to a report of the U.S. Government Accountability Office, 83 of 100 major American corporations and 63 of the 100 largest contractors with ties to the government have subsidiaries in countries that are generally considered tax havens. Coca-Cola, Procter and Gamble, General Motors, Intel, FedEx, and Sprint all have subsidiaries in the Cayman Islands. In the Cayman Islands major financial organizations such as UBS and Goldman Sachs and leading audit firms such as Ernst and Young, KPMG, Pricewaterhouse-Coopers, and Deloitte Touche Tohmatsu offer financial services to their clients and "investors."

We are not talking about the income of underground syndicates that smuggle weapons or trade in drugs or humans. The overwhelming majority of the money circulating in and through offshore havens consists of income from legal business, obtained by respected companies and people who shape to a large extent public opinion and the political landscape of their countries.

In fact, from nearly every possible viewpoint—corporate finance transparency, soundness of public finance, macroeconomic stability, fairness in treating various businesses, and so on—there is not a single justification for Western governments to tolerate "special" jurisdictions that sap tremendous tax revenues from economic "mainlands." Because financial information on tax havens is hard to obtain, data differ on the losses that they inflict on other economies. But every G-7 country (or G-8, if we include Russia, which suffers the same economic drain) loses at least dozens of billions of dollars; some lose more than a hundred billion. Moreover, the names of the overwhelming majority of corporations and people evading taxation in their home countries through offshore companies are well known. (As U.S. President Barack Obama said, "You've got a building in the Cayman Islands that supposedly houses 12,000 corporations. That's either the biggest building or the biggest tax scam on record.")

But calls for coordinated efforts to put an end to a phenomenon that is clearly detrimental to fiscal systems of Western countries go nowhere. And even though pleas for cooperation on this issue have been more emphatic during the financial crisis, and President Obama has threatened harsh measures against corporations that register their subsidiaries and associates in such jurisdictions, so far all attempts to block the flow of capital to offshore jurisdictions have been futile.

So why are those jurisdictions not only tolerated but implicitly blessed by financial and government authorities in the West? I regularly am told by influential people that the transfer of money into the "shadows" of "gray zones," like most human vices, is far easier to control, at least formally, than to suppress. But the only explanation that looks plausible to me is that the interests holding their money in offshore jurisdictions simply have sufficient political influence in their home countries to protect their own interests.

But that's not all there is to it. I am convinced that the battle against offshore havens would have been an integral part of political agendas, implemented more seriously and perhaps even successfully, but for the shift in the structure of Western economies to the "new," largely virtual, economy, which blurred the transparency of financial flows.

Nor can these shifts in both the structure and the nature of the world's leading economies fail to have affected public morality. As we have seen, activities serving the public good, satisfying reasonable needs of citizens, and contributing to the prosperity of communities, localities, and nations help maintain the set of moral values that has persevered through the centuries and laid the foundation of industrial development in modern times. The relation of most activities in the "new economy" to consumer welfare and public prosperity is tenuous. The talk of "greedy bankers" and "financial capitalism" that suddenly broke out at the outset of the crisis didn't appear out of nowhere and for no reason. Underlying this talk was a longstanding perception that speculation in securities has no moral justification to begin, even apart from the use of special techniques to lure ordinary savers and institutions that hold clients' or public money (like pension, insurance, or trust funds) into throwing the money into the hands of gamblers in the financial sector.

The same applies to traders in "high-tech innovations," who rarely can produce evidence that they actually bear costs necessitated by serious R&D activities, or that their products have real material value for individual consumers and the public at large when compared with traditional consumer goods.

It's clear to me that the long-term shift of Western economies from mining and manufacturing industries to the services sector—and within that sector, toward services of intermediate or derivative nature, the utility of which for general well-being and prosperity becomes progressively vague and undetectable—has had a negative effect on the state of public morality. Public morality inevitably suffers when we create services of unclear purpose and value, and when we manipulate human needs and desires, thereby bringing rates of return incomparable to those in sectors indispensable for securing basic needs of a community or nation. Just as inevitably those rates of return further stimulate the young and bright to seek employment in sectors contributing to further "virtualization" of Western economies.

Debt

One result of major shifts in economies of developed countries over the past few decades is excessive credit growth, which in turn has its own consequences. In this process the United States has been the main driver. The habit of living on borrowed means has pervaded not only the state sector, from the federal government down through municipalities, but also the public at large, with aggregate debt close to $13 trillion in 2008. At the same time a consumer credit boom has affected almost all the economically active population strata in other developed countries.

We have witnessed the start of a collapse in the traditional distribution of roles between large sectors in the economy, where the household sector was a net creditor and nonfinancial corporations were the main borrowers, with the financial sector acting as the intermediary between the two. In the household sector, the savings culture formed by European tradition over centuries was replaced by a consumer boom typified by the formula "Why wait for tomorrow if you can consume today?" Or, as one advertising slogan put it, "You have only just thought of something, and we're already prepared to extend you a loan to buy it."

The housing bubble in the United States that nearly brought down the banking system was in fact simply the logical outcome of a protracted gradual easing of requirements by banks for potential borrowers. This was in turn attributable to stable growth in household incomes and the size of aggregate credit and real estate that served as collateral. In such circumstances even rising defaults on loans did not slow credit growth as a whole, as the sale of collateral in most cases enabled banks to avoid significant losses, and resulting losses created serious problems in the context of aggregate lending data in the banking sector.

The fall in the savings ratios in developed countries, which occurred at a time of progressive deindustrialization and a general decay in the transparency of capital flows in the "virtual" economy, was the context and simultaneously the result of unprecedented expansion in consumer lending. These processes developed in parallel, thereby mutually supporting each other. For example, growth in the share of the services sector objectively increased the share of wages in the gross product, reducing the ratio of consumed capital in its structure and stimulating growth of the share of final consumption in gross national expenditure. At the same time this was also attributable to a general reduction in the tax burden that resulted from new opportunities to manipulate financial flows in the corporate sector and to thereby "optimize" tax liabilities. Growth in personal disposable income created new opportunities to stimulate consumption of a public who believed that perceptible growth in personal income was a sign of sustainable prosperity and consequently had less incentive to save. At the same time, the growth in personal income eased household access to consumer credit, which in turn acted as another saving disincentive.

Simultaneously, however, the growing propensity to consume in developed countries objectively weakened the funding base of the financial sector, reducing (in proportion to growth in aggregate income) the inflow of cash to banks and retail investment funds. However, the latter perceived new opportunities to attract more funds from developing countries, where people sought protection from instability in their own countries by willingly investing in financial assets in developed countries. This propensity was leveraged in turn by the U.S. government, which was accorded opportunities to finance its budget and trade deficit by attracting increasing capital from poorer countries. At the same time, private financial institutions benefited just as much, using this money to finance consumption in the United States and other countries where a consumer economy had taken hold in the second half of the twentieth century.

The debt burden on the economies of developed countries consistently grew, which undermined the stability of those economies. On the other hand, indebtedness to the financial sector of households and governments in the developed economies increased in proportion to incomes (or GDP).

That too must certainly have affected public and business morality at least in two important aspects. First, it affected the sense of responsibility of economic agents, especially of households. When debt exceeds certain limits (different for each case, so not quantifiable as a set of indicators), any further growth of the debt's size or decline in the prospects of its eventual repayment becomes the creditor's rather than the debtor's concern. When people in similar financial positions start borrowing irresponsibly, with nobody in the government or in the financial sector raising concern over possible consequences, the traditional responsibility governing personal finance may be diluted. Besides, if governments borrow heavily on the premise that by the time their debt matures their revenues will grow, why shouldn't individual households act in the same way?

Second, when debt of governments and households becomes a way of life rather than a short-term solution to temporary problems, when it turns into an attempt (often unconscious) to consume more than you can earn and transfer related burdens onto other people (future generations, poorer nations that invest in Western government bonds, or, as in a case of high inflation, all those willing to save), it undermines ethical principles that promise fair reward for hard toil, responsible behavior, and self-support.

Credit

Nevertheless, as debt grew and nothing dire happened, people started to believe that the modern economy was somehow able to function unimpaired with increasing credit and diverse forms of debt. Governments would leverage their privileges in the financial sector with loans to erase any signs of incipient diminution of production or a deteriorating balance of trade, constantly testing the dependence of their economies on bank credits by continually raising borrowing levels. On each occasion they discovered that they were achieving their goals without provoking an upsurge in inflation. Meanwhile, the general growth in income and living standards at a time of moderate price growth was reducing the load of the debt burden on business and the public. Consequently, as it seemed and still seems to many economists, a relatively secure method for supporting long-term economic growth had passed the test. This development was politically acceptable for all influential groups and created no significant social tension, at least in Western countries.

One could even say that credit has to some extent assumed mythic qualities. The ability to obtain everything now and pay at some date in the future without experiencing significant stress appeared closer than ever to realization. At the outset of their economically active life, people had a chance to move into their own homes, refurbish them, enjoy a high level of consumption, all on credit, with nominal repayments due at a time when household income would be far higher, so that the burden of debt payments would be moderate relative to overall price and income growth.

This expectation implied that borrowers could improve their living standards thanks to savers. These savers, meanwhile, voluntarily forwent present consumption (and, to the extent that their savings would be depreciated by inflation and a general rise in living standards, some future consumption as well) to the benefit of active borrowers or financial intermediaries. The intermediaries were the biggest winners, but active borrowers also benefited considerably from enormous credit expansion in the decades preceding the crisis. Not that people who borrowed are to blame for the Great Recession; the guilt rests largely with the monetary authorities who insisted on keeping interest rates low and credit restrictions lax to prevent growth of the GDP from stalling. The authorities knew that the growth they were encouraging in consumer demand was largely artificial and could lead to instability. Nevertheless, ordinary households that were lured by unsound economic policy into expanding their consumption beyond the limits of their reasonable income expectations also bear a share of moral responsibility.

Increased consumption further stimulated expansion of the financial sector, as well as deindustrialization and virtualization of the economy. The savers in this model made up a diminishing and less politically active segment of the population, while the winners were the growing masses and more influential participants in the process, so this model met no perceptible political resistance, and in effect still hasn't.

Liabilities in the banking system represent the only material limitation on the general desire to inflate credit. This limitation can be relaxed in part by the monetary authorities, which can replenish the banking system's liquidity via increasing money supply. However, their ability to do so is hampered by the threat that inflation will accelerate beyond a certain threshold considered safe. Therefore the growth in the debt economy over recent decades was to a large extent financed by an alternative source: the inflow of capital from "new industrial" countries—emerging markets—and from the rich in poor countries and regions. Exact data on the size of this inflow do not exist. However, the figure runs into hundreds of billions, perhaps trillions of dollars, which would appear to have played a key role over the past few decades in the uncontrollable expansion of credit and debt-laden economies.

Rent

Let us highlight one consequence of this inflow: the growing role of intellectual rent in the distribution of income and property both between economic agents within national economies and between nations.

Here we must make a slight digression. Over the period of several decades most items of mass consumption have had costs increasingly disproportionate to the production costs. Even comparatively simple products came to contain a cost component presented as compensation for research and development, including the development of new materials, technologies, and types of equipment used in their production. (I have addressed elsewhere the question of the legitimacy of these costs.) This component can easily account for 90 percent or more of the price of products that are presented specifically as "high tech," for example, medical and health products, new electronic gadgets, or specific industrial materials.

Compensation for all indirect expenses allegedly incurred might be specified as a corresponding portion of fixed costs or might be included in the price of materials and components used in the production of the product. When, for example, a producer of electronic gadgets obtains components used in assembling the product, prices of these components include costs allegedly incurred in R&D, testing, obtaining intellectual property rights, and the like. But an increasing share of costs is presented as formal remuneration of the developer or of the owners of intellectual property rights paid as various licensing fees and royalties.

Over the past two or three decades this phenomenon has been assuming ever more distinctive forms. For instance, the price of any good or service employing computer technology (more than half of everything produced in the world) indirectly includes payments made to the owners of rights to software. As nearly all manufacturers are using more and more complicated and multifaceted telecommunications services, payments to owners of telecommunications technologies constitute an ever increasing part of the cost of production.

Virtually all production activities even outside the developed world are performed nowadays with the use of borrowed funds. As a result, the cost of a product includes interest or other associated debt payments, which include not only payments to the owners of the borrowed capital but also huge expenses for the maintenance of the infrastructure of modern financial markets and the legal framework and media networks that service them.

Costs formally specified as "marketing expenses" include the cost of maintaining various departments to study the markets, as well as payments to the owners of titles to corresponding information, and the technologies used to process this information. Though that has always been the case with new and innovative products, the relative size of these elements of cost has been steadily growing over recent decades, if only because the sheer size of market infrastructure has increased visibly, and material costs of its maintenance must somehow be covered by the price of the end product.

Finally, advertising costs have grown to exceed even the most audacious predictions. In contrast, expenses to inform potential consumers of the technology, consumption, and acquisition of the product account for a relatively small proportion of total advertising costs. Most of these expenses are spent on brand building or on the creation of consumer demand (real or fabricated) for a product of a specified manufacturer or seller. In other words, the consumer is paying more and more for the image or a brand, a virtual component, rather than for the actual product, with sales revenues remitted through title to the advertised trademarks or brands to the owners of this specific intellectual property. This is the case especially in the oligopolistic markets, like premium-brand home electronics, cigarettes, beverages, or cosmetic products, in which world brand names bring billions of dollars in revenues to their owners.

If we add up all the price components that relate to intellectual costs and/or title ownership, we see that they are starting to outweigh such traditional components as fair compensation for labor and capital used in production and valued at market prices. Accordingly, they are beginning to dominate the distribution pattern of sales revenues, directing an ever growing part of it to formal or de facto owners of titles to intellectual products.

Of course, even now goods devoid of these components are produced and consumed all over the world. For example, consumers of milk from a farm somewhere in Africa do not pay anything to global brand owners or to the developers of telecommunications technologies. It is also highly unlikely that tourists handing over their dollars in the middle of nowhere for fake souvenirs are paying anything to the owners of any kind of intellectual property. Nevertheless, it is absolutely clear that the increase in proportion of revenues from intellectual factors is a general trend.

Trademarks

Consequently, consumers in the West already pay regularly and systematically not only for the services of labor and capital, for the use of natural resources, and to remunerate managers and entrepreneurs for their activities and risks. They also pay for access in some form or another to intellectual products created at some time in the past—real (technologies) or imaginary (image trademarks)—rights owned today by individuals or organizations. Though specific figures are never disclosed, it is an open secret that production costs of branded goods (which are regularly outsourced to producers from so-called low-cost countries) often constitute less than 10 percent of the end price paid by consumer, the rest being distributed between holders of rights to the brand name, who usually also hold control over use of certain production technologies, and distribution channels.

This is true as well (and perhaps to a larger degree) for the poorer countries. Consumption there (among those with more than a subsistence level of income) is also being transformed through enhanced intellectual-technological and virtual-image components. Thus the international spread of antiglobalist movements is not accidental. Antiglobalist sentiment grows whenever Microsoft, Coca-Cola, Toyota, Gillette, or McDonald's (to name a few randomly chosen examples) uses advertising and technology to exploit expanding consumption anywhere in the world as a source of un-earned (rent) income. Consumers have no choice but to pay for titles to trademarks and such nebulous assets as long-established business relations, brand recognition, and other intangible assets, because these costs are hidden on the price tag.

In other words, the past few decades have been marked by a continuing shift in the relationship between various sources of revenues and wealth. An increasingly substantial share represents the title to accumulated intangible assets. Past investments, which entitle their owners to earn a kind of historical rent, guarantee today a much higher rate of return than can be earned by investing in production facilities.[4]

How does this topic relate to the issue of morality in business? The changes described in this chapter mean that the increasing share of incomes derived by business owners represents not remuneration for their organizational skills, business talents, force of vision, or the risks they undertake. Instead, it represents a kind of fixed rent that owners extract from their rights to intellectual products, often of dubious value, with the view of their ability to satisfy reasonable (or "real," if we use Marcuse's term) needs of a typical consumer or to initiate and facilitate economic development, justified by an established set of values. Considering that the amounts of time, energy, and natural resources in an economic system are naturally limited, a trade-off exists between the amount spent on brand building or on imposing specific wants on consumers and the amount used to build up material infrastructure or produce goods and services that help upgrade physical conditions directly affecting the well-being of communities and nations.

Emergence of a powerful source of revenue that originates at best from past achievements, at worst merely from a supplier's ability to impose certain views and preferences onto people's minds, could be viewed as one of the factors that lies beneath the general slackening of mechanisms of self-regulation and self-discipline in business classes. Though the role of this factor in bringing about the Great Recession could hardly be treated as major or direct, it certainly forms an important part of the scene where the crisis unfolded.

The fact that nearly all "virtual" revenues go to the wealthier part of the world also has clear moral implications. The tendency for such revenues to concentrate in the West is natural, since titles to the overwhelming majority of intangible assets are held and will continue to be held by major multinational corporations, whose origins and main activity are in the developed world. These corporations, which accumulate revenues attributable to intangible properties, expand the economies of their home countries with those revenues, thus expanding the gap between the world's haves and have-nots. If there is a moral component to the ideal of narrowing social, economic, and cultural gaps that divide the modern world, then such a component exists as well in movements that drive the world farther from this ideal.

Implications and Risks

Moreover, some indirect effects of these major shifts in the world economy, as well as associated risks, carry even deeper moral implications.

First, we could theoretically view as a purely technical change that has no material impact on people's psychology the shift of the economies of developed countries toward the services sector, especially toward services directly or indirectly related to the financial sector, and the production of so-called high-tech goods, for which actual production costs account for an immaterial proportion of the price. However, this theory cannot hold up to scrutiny.

In fact, the financial markets, in particular speculation on stock exchanges, have traditionally been considered a favored area for opportunists, lovers of free and easy money, and outright frauds. The image of a greedy banker or financial gambler who has no roots or moral compass and flouts such mundane concepts as honest labor and prudence was one of the favorite topics of the media when the Great Recession became everybody's concern.

The extent to which this image reflects reality is a matter for discussion. As a field to which to apply one's intellect, creativity, and effort, the financial sector is as good as any other, and there is no reason to single it out as a source of selfishness or wrongdoing.[5] On the other hand, unlike in many other spheres, here only a thin line separates risky legal but ethically questionable transactions from illegal action. Violations of internal rules and regulations that were technically legal can crystallize into a criminal case if the violations lead to serious damage for a company or third parties. The categories of "knowingly" and "deliberately," which often play a key role in classifying the actions and culpability of a specific individual, are difficult to prove and in many cases virtually impossible to define. The definition of insider information, the use of which often separates a legal action from an illegal one, often requires more legal knowledge that the participants in such transactions are likely to have. Most well-known examples of success in finance are built in part on actions not far from the line demarcating dishonest business practice.

When compared with other lines of business, a much higher percentage of transactions in finance may be categorized as zero-sum games. The income of people working in this sector is generated far more than elsewhere by the losses incurred by other participants—indeed, such losses are considered an indispensable condition. In other words, the elements of cooperation and organized joint creativity, which often enable people to apply and realize the best aspects of their nature, are far rarer here.

Furthermore, speculative transactions by their very nature bear little relation to the creation and productive use of basic economic resources. Arbitrage is a useful activity from the perspective of the normal functioning of the market and to some extent promotes its optimization in terms of the overall activity of the contemporary financial sector, it plays a comparatively small role.[6] This also holds true for insurance in its classic form, which reduces existing commercial risks by distributing them, without generating new serious risks capable of destabilizing and circumventing the market system. However, nowadays an increasing portion of activity in the financial sector can be summed up as attempts to redistribute resources committed to the market through the design of new financial products, the qualities and benefits of which are less obvious, and accordingly are further removed from the useful function initially inherent in this sector: to optimize use of economic resources by mobilizing the funds of passive savers and using this money to finance active constructive business activity in growing industries.

As I sought to indicate earlier, the concentration of an ever increasing proportion of human and intellectual resources in the financial and related sectors inevitably creates even more distance between the end users of different types of financial and related services (for example, between individual investors and ultimate borrowers of funds) and accordingly creates a more favorable environment for the market players in this sector to secure an ever larger proportion of total output by rendering its composition and structure more and more sophisticated and abstract.

Indeed, if one compares the standard offerings and descriptions of financial products advertised by trust and investment companies to those of thirty or forty years ago, the progress in their number and sophistication is evident. And certainly this expansion diluted the content and meaning of the activities in question from their original economic rationale and moral justification—that is, from "allocating productive capital more efficiently, ultimately generating benefits for the society as a whole."[7]

This renders the task of applying moral criteria to such activity even harder, other than in terms of compliance with the law. At the same time, the legality of some transactions is becoming less clear because of the increasingly complex nature of their structure and content, something I will consider in more detail later.

Ultimately, activity yielding imperceptible benefits for society is accounting for an increasing share of business as a whole.[8] For example, the U.S. financial sector increased its share of GDP from 13 percent in 1970 to 20 percent in 2007, and its share of total corporate profits grew even higher—to around 40 percent, according to some estimates.[9]

It is important to note the following: regardless of whether the legal authorities target businesses in this sector, and regardless of the participants' declarations of blamelessness before the law, public trust in business as a whole will inevitably deteriorate as this sector increases in importance, if only because the public implicitly believes that this sector of business has come to operate largely out of reach of public control and the rules of accepted morality.

References to "financial capitalism" among the political elite at the beginning of 2009, as if it were a special type of economy, as opposed to classical capitalism (in other words, manufacturing and industry), did not appear out of the blue. Such talk is closely tied to assertions about the need for the moral rehabilitation of the modern economic system, and it reflects the public perception of the dubious nature of the vast array of businesses that have grown and continue to grow on the basis of financial intermediation.

This issue has been summarized with great clarity in several statements made at a two-day conference, "New World, New Capitalism," in January 2009, organized by French President Nicolas Sarkozy, former British Prime Minister Tony Blair, and German Chancellor Angela Merkel. According to Sarkozy, for example, "Purely financial capitalism has perverted the logic of capitalism. . . . It is amoral. It is a system where the logic of the market excuses everything." Elsewhere he was quoted, "It's a system where wealth goes to the wealthy, where work is devalued, where production is devalued, where entrepreneurial spirit is devalued." Sarkozy was echoed by Tony Blair, who called for a new financial order based on "values other than the maximum short-term profit." A year later, addressing the World Economic Forum annual meeting in January 2010, Sarkozy observed: "We will only save capitalism by reforming it, by making it more moral."[10]

When such pronouncements are made by people capable of catching the public mood and assessments of the active part of society, they indicate an increasingly widespread public perception. In this case the perception is that it is fundamentally wrong for the economy to depart from production of sought-after goods and focus instead on speculative structures and financial technologies that make it possible to redistribute income without any evident benefit for society.

Magical "Innovations"

While the financial sector has attracted the most attention during the Great Recession, indirect negative implications for the disciplining role of public morality in economic life could be found to some extent in yet another structural change in the economies of developed countries—an increase in technological effectiveness and "innovation."

As I have written, the commonly accepted vision of technological progress as a transformational force bringing about social progress seems to me to a large degree specious and hypocritical. Of course, no one would deny that technological advances over the past century have created conditions indispensable for the existence of most of the modern economy. However, many things claimed as technological "innovations" and portrayed as driving forces for present and future growth in reality bear little relation to technological progress, if that progress is defined as a tool for understanding and transforming physical reality, or for developing and utilizing human potential. Moreover, in many practical cases this pseudoprogress serves as a basis for yet another form of unearned income, which could be called "innovation royalty."[11]

Many advertised "innovations" represent little more than marketing ploys to promote new or allegedly new products. For the most part, this involves the mass market, where the role of irrational, induced concepts is by definition vast. Truly revolutionary ideas and inventions do exist, inventions that have given people powerful tools to realize their intellectual and creative potential. Computer technology, the Internet, new materials with unique characteristics, biotechnologies—all these will of course go down as some of the greatest achievements in human history. However, in terms of the money brought to specific companies and individuals, those great inventions at best only slightly outperform such "innovations" as a new recipe for a soft drink or a new handset design, which has no recognizable differences for 99 percent of consumers.

I doubt whether exact data could be compiled to quantify revenue each new product brought to those who held control over its distribution, but much indirect evidence substantiates the general principle. The list of world brands with the biggest capitalization, for example, shows that a string of soft drinks developed by Coca-Cola, or shaving accessories by Gillette, or handset models by Nokia secure for these brands capitalization comparable to that of Intel or IBM. In terms of profitability, development of space or other frontier technologies could never rival development of new collections in fashion industry, with Louis Vuitton easily outperforming Apple or Boeing.

But the problem lies not only in the disparity between the scale of innovation and its market value but also in the nature of "innovation" as such. Consumers not only pay for the real products of technological progress; often they pay (or rather are coerced into paying) for "progress" that is nonexistent, or at least far shy of advertising claims. Products are manufactured with the shortest possible shelf life, in sharp contrast to the case twenty or one hundred years ago. Models five to seven years old are no longer serviced. Upgraded computer application programs are incompatible with earlier operating systems, forcing the consumer to acquire new systems, which are not necessarily more efficient. Numerous lawsuits against Microsoft cite these monopolistic practices.[12]

We do not know how many great minds worked on the next "unique formula" for shampoo or "improved handset designs"—this is a commercial secret. However, over the past few decades the share of national income redistributed to the beneficiaries of "innovative" companies has grown substantially. The increasing influence of advertising made this redistribution possible. So the media, which serve as conduits for advertising, also catch some of the "high-tech" and "innovation" royalty. However, the lion's share of it goes to big business.

The growing share of this segment in the economy of developed countries inevitably has affected the moral climate of business. However the people profiting from these innovations may evaluate their own contributions, they receive incomes, if not fortunes, that are clearly incommensurate with the effort and risk involved. Many of these people may feel that they are justified in receiving their rewards from the system they have mastered. At the same time, some must realize that their prosperity depends less on their special talents than on the power of influence on consumer behavior, which incorporates misleading information about the attributes of a product. At least some of those involved must feel a certain moral discomfort regarding the foundation of their careers and prosperity, which will in turn have an impact on their behavior in business.[13]

Status

The system of selling "air" instead of the high-tech component of a product is not limited to marketing executives and salespeople. Consumers also play an active role in the system. As the targets of the system, they consciously obtain the "inflated" products, but they are acquiring image and status rather than air. In general they don't care about the truth of the statements on the innovative component as long as the product delivers the promised prestige.

Expensive attributes of status, such as a Breguet watch or a gold Parker pen, have been around for a long time. Unlike today's electronic gadgets that replace each other at lightning speed, however, those luxury goods represented a benchmark for technological perfection and virtually never became obsolete. The acquisition of such a product was a milestone in one's life.

Over the past twenty years, companies seeking to capitalize on fashions for high-tech products have targeted a large stratum of consumers from different social backgrounds, from business leaders and government officials to rank-and-file office staff, urging them to support the "sale of air."[14]

However, the desire to buy status (all the newest and the "coolest") and keep up with their peers can push people to make even more empty-headed acts than spending half their wages on the next version of an electronic toy.

It seems to me that considerations of status played a key role in the growth of wild demand for cheap, unsecured mortgages. This is only a guess, and it may meet objections. However, my life's experience as a politician, which has involved mixing extensively with people of different social status and educational background, makes me believe the following. If it becomes possible to buy housing in a prestigious neighborhood, and some people take advantage of the opportunity, their peers will also buy, with no consideration of economic risks—they feel the pressure "to keep up with the Joneses," despite any rational objections. Meanwhile, the thought that the global market, the state, and in general people responsible for society's stability will somehow take care of any problems becomes for many people a convenient excuse for abdicating responsibility for possible consequences of risky financial decisions, for example, the acquisition of a new house that actually belongs to the bank.

A good example of such attitudes infiltrating much of the population is the Greek crisis in the euro zone. In Greece, hundreds of thousands of people vehemently protested against austerity measures designed to cut an intolerably huge budget deficit. One underlying sentiment behind those protests was that those who actually benefited from excessive borrowing and consumption should not have to pay for the ensuing troubles. If the country's finances were a shambles, the EU (or multinational financial institutions, or people managing the global economy) should take care of the problem; those who had been given a chance to spend unearned money had no intention of accepting blame or making sacrifices. I can't help believing that this crisis reflects the general trend of taking an easygoing attitude toward financial obligations, a trend born of the increasing abstraction of inflated activities of the financial sector, which can obscure the ultimate borrower.

Indulgences

Strictly speaking, the vulnerability exploited by shady businesses built on disregard for long-term consequences to the economy and society and on speculation on the weaknesses of human nature is nothing new. This niche has always existed in various manifestations, not limited to the financial sector. Real estate, public investment, construction, and the production and distribution of various health and cosmetic products, for example, have always provided openings for shady business operatives.

These niches have always been filled by people whose mindset privileges profit over morality; some, in order to adapt to this type of business, may have nurtured a stance that does not even reflect their real characters. However, this niche has expanded in recent years, with an inevitable effect on the general business climate. From what I see and hear from my contacts and in discussions with other interested people, as well as from my own daily experience, I have a strong feeling that many members of the political, intellectual, and business elite have come to disregard differences between constructive business and intellectual speculation with money— between socially productive and socially irresponsible business—and to display general tolerance toward intellectual slyness bordering on deceit. Perceiving the latter as just another intellectual indulgence is becoming rather common in the business community, and also in intellectual strata feeding off these niches. I cannot substantiate this feeling with figures or statistical data, but if it does reflect the modern elite's state of mind, that must be related to the expansion over the past three decades of niches for intellectually deceptive business practices. It should come as no surprise that past decades have seen a wider acceptance of the idea that all business must be treated equally and similarly and that no discrimination based on social significance should be tolerated, an attitude based on a strict libertarian interpretation of the consumer's right to make a free choice, even if that choice makes the consumer vulnerable to deceit. Politicians who promoted the idea that "all businesses are equal," that any interference with market competition based on social importance is illegitimate, have gained influence in both Europe and the United States. Consequently, the notion that the only duty of business is to be profitable, that other functions can be delegated to other institutions, has achieved wider popularity than ever before, and I consider this notion to be an integral part of Realeconomik thinking.[15]

But society cannot be indifferent to the conditions when it offers intellectual indulgence to those who profit from public ignorance. Such indulgence inevitably leads to the slackening of public constraints on individual vices and weaknesses. To put it crudely, just as a victorious coup d'état is called a revolution, cynicism and deceit come to be considered honest business if the people making a career on this basis become influential and respected members of society.

The gradual erosion of moral boundaries was certainly facilitated by the trend toward the virtualization of business and the separation between a growing proportion of economic activity and the production base and the requirements of the consumer. When it is no longer clear why a specific financial transaction takes place and who is the beneficiary, the concept of "moral constraint" becomes as virtual as the business itself. Moreover, as I have stated, the virtualization of business implies that the concepts of productivity and cost effectiveness have lost all practical meaning for a significant proportion of the economic activities, which also makes it impossible to apply a criterion such as efficiency to determine the worthiness of a business.

The tendency toward virtualization is complemented by the declining transparency of financial flows (I refer not to formal accountability, which may have increased in volume and scope, but rather clarity in the meaning and underlying aspects of transactions) and the growing role of offshore transactions. After the Gazprom group experienced fast growth in the scope and complexity of financial flows in the 1990s, leading to complications in the system of relations within the group, members of senior management admitted privately to me at the time that both the government, as formal owner of the group, and the managers themselves had at some point lost the ability to understand the complex network of financial and management connections within the group, let alone to manage the company.[16] Nobody could form in his head a single clear picture of how—and, more important, why and in whose interests—billions of dollars were moved in financial flows. Nobody could understand the final goal of the numerous real and fictitious deals that theoretically should have reflected the interests of the group as a whole and its owner, the government.

Something similar was happening at major business groups in Western economies, if only because the increasing complexity and the use of sophisticated software had to be accompanied by a reduction in actual transparency and manageability.

Wake-Up Call

This general picture is related to the fate of the system of moral guidelines. First, because the government's ability to regulate business activity (allegedly in the interests of the public) becomes more limited as the organization of business becomes more complex and intertwined with various technologies, hence more opaque and difficult to see through. Moreover, government regulation is less stringent than many people realize, and is effective only when it reflects and is reinforced by the psychological and moral principles ingrained in society. History shows us that strong national leaders, driven by noble or ignoble intentions, repeatedly have done all they could to force their people to abide by the law. Rarely were these attempts successful. Laws work satisfactorily only when they are reinforced by the momentum of daily life lived according to certain principles spontaneously evolved over time by a society—principles that encompass what we call morality. If such principles are absent—for example, they did not fully evolve or were eroded or destroyed during historical cataclysms—then no system of coercion can force society to accept a law foisted upon it as a source of behavioral norms; nor will its citizens adhere to such a law in daily life.

But the power of moral norms is also limited. These norms became entrenched as a set of rules used to regulate the lives of comparatively simple communities, where everyone's life is known to other community members and the actions of each individual are constantly set against the moral perceptions of other members. Thus the larger and more complex a society, the broader the social circle and the greater the number of important actions that are not subject to social control, the greater the burden on the strength of moral norms and constraints and accordingly the more these norms must be reinforced by the power and effectiveness of public opinion and the state's ability as a force to consolidate that opinion.

From this perspective, structural shifts over the past few decades have made the conditions for outside control, including moral control, more difficult. First, an excessive part of the economy has become virtually opaque and even simply inaccessible to public oversight, whereas the privileges and bonuses seized by the violators of norms have become so large that the system of moral constraints has become overloaded. The Great Recession could be seen as a manifestation of this condition, and it required the acute danger of chaos in financial markets and the resulting protracted slump to wake up public opinion to the need to "put the house in order" in the financial sector and to apply moral constraints to actions (and incomes) of its top executives.

Moreover, all the logic of the "new economy" has in recent decades evolved in such a way that business success has become inseparable from moral compromises, which resulted in extremely unpleasant "surprises" as the full dimensions of the crisis became clear.

Second, in the new environment the economy lost all benchmarks for development. The super profits of the financial sector cannot be considered such a benchmark, while the concepts of productivity and efficient use of economic resources have been diluted by the increasing share of intangible assets that now account for 90 percent or more of the price of the end product.

A strange and difficult situation is emerging for the developed world. On the one hand, mainstream business resembles more and more a black box, where opaque technologies are used to produce goods and services that are called innovative and consequently are sold at prices that bear little relation to verifiable costs. In these circumstances, it becomes virtually impossible to apply any efficiency criteria other than revenue and profit, leaving no room for moral assessments and constraints. There is a temptation to call everything that yields large profits cost effective and therefore useful and even moral (or at least morally neutral). This is the direction in which global business has been evolving over the past two decades.

It may seem counterintuitive, but the cost effectiveness of business activity (not to mention the public good), as I have explained, is directly dependent on the existence of moral standards in society and business and on their stability and effectiveness; and that is why both society and the economy are paying a high price for financial and moral opacity. The interdependence of business success and moral standards is established through the mechanism of trust between economic agents, without which the success of market capitalism is impossible in principle. In the second part of this book, I hope to show that public morality is not reduced just to this role but has a far broader and multifaceted character.

The consequence of this mutual dependency is that any dilution of moral constraint poses a threat to public interest and goals and also to sustainable economic growth, something well demonstrated in the Great Recession. It should be understood that the crisis is simply one episode on a long journey. It has triggered thoughts about how to guarantee the requisite conditions for sustainable, healthy growth in the economy. But for the time being there is no reason to believe that the world has changed or will change once this crisis comes to an end. None of the shifts in modern capitalism I have mentioned is the result of someone's evil intentions; all represent instead the evolution of our contemporary world over time. It appears that these shifts will continue even after the economies of developed countries have recovered from the recession and even after the reconstruction of the world financial system, if and when that happens. For now, no agreement exists internationally on realistic recipes to alter the direction of current developments. Moreover, it is unclear whether influential forces in the world are actually seeking such changes and whether they have the requisite political will to undertake steps to start setting the world economy on a different course.

The impact of shifts in the world economy on the efficacy of moral constraints highlights yet another fact. Current relations in the world economy, in which the developed world increasingly enjoys unearned income resulting from control over overwhelming share of rent-producing intangible assets—a phenomenon that itself constitutes a new moral irritant—have moved beyond the market economy and now play a role in international relations. I will discuss these relations in the following chapter.

4

International Relations, 1980s–2008

Putting Self-Interest First

In this chapter I shall focus on developments in international relations over the past two decades and link the evolution of these relations to my main topic, which is the changing role of moral restraints in today's global economy as a by-product of Realeconomik beliefs.

Divided World

From the 1960s through the 1980s, it was commonly held that the gap between rich and poor countries was an abnormal phenomenon and that the developed world should work toward eliminating this gap, partly to forward its own interests—to guarantee stability in the Third World, curb the flow of refugees, and expand markets, for example—but primarily out of moral considerations.

As the idea of progress—economic, social, and political—was the key priority for the intellectual elite in the second half of the twentieth century, the conventional wisdom (in public, at any rate) was that it was demeaning to humanity to tolerate the existence of profound, depressive, and self-perpetuating poverty in enormous territories, even entire regions. During this period a number of international programs were established to promote development, primarily under the aegis of the United Nations, while international financial institutions sought to help, to the extent that they could, and the governments of developed countries adopted their own aid programs for developing countries. As a result of stubborn work spanning decades, the markets of developed countries opened to products from developing countries, giving some hope for long-term economic competitiveness.

Over the past twenty to twenty-five years, however, the situation has altered radically. The protective and compassionate attitude of the developed world toward the economic woes of developing countries that characterized the previous period has been replaced by flagrant indifference or barely concealed irritation. This change in attitude may in part have been a reaction to the behavior of ruling elites in some countries who themselves displayed indifference to national problems and unwillingness to make any effort to modernize and encourage economic growth. If the developed world's recalcitrance had been applied to such countries only, it might have had some justification. In practice, however, even countries that achieved considerable progress toward industrialization and internationalization of their economies came to be treated more with jealousy and apprehension than with encouragement and support. Even reports by Western think tanks and statements by highly placed officials now urge developing countries to rely on market mechanisms rather than aid in order to increase their economic efficiency and ultimately their affluence. And during informal exchanges of opinions, when strict rules of political correctness could be bent, cool allusions to existing (and probably insurmountable) gaps and barriers, coupled with resentment over insistent demands by the developing countries for more aid and privileges, came to be heard more often than compassion or promises of assistance.

For all the political correctness of public and official statements from the Western world, the general impression has become that the goal of surmounting the gulf in development levels in different parts of the world economy is no longer a priority, or at least has been deferred indefinitely.[1] Putting aside such basic elements as humanitarian and food aid, the Western world has preferred to rely on elementary natural mechanisms to close the gap between itself and the less fortunate peoples. It was assumed that the low cost of a number of key resources, primarily labor, would enable developing countries to increase their international competitiveness and thereby attract new investment and finance. As a result the unspoken assumption was that a reduction in the gulf in living standards and incomes between the countries of the so-called golden billion and the majority of the population in the rest of the world would be a long-term trend, resulting, in the end, in the virtual disappearance of chronic poverty zones.[2]

Admittedly, while the manufacturing industry was still playing the role of the main driver of economic growth in the developed world, integration of manufacturing industries in developing countries into the global capitalist economy met with significant difficulties. Nevertheless, they were considered primarily technical problems that could be handled by facilitating the restructuring of the economies of the developed countries into "postindustrial" economies—that is, into economies dominated by service industries as opposed to manufacturing.

As the developed world engaged in building such postindustrial economies, these problems indeed began to abate. It turned out that the transfer of a substantial part of manufacturing production to the more advanced countries of the former Third World increased the cost effectiveness of business activity of a "new economy."

The term "new economy" itself lacks an established clear-cut definition. Depending on the context, it implies different sets of industries and areas of business activities, as one can easily see from the regular stream of business news and analysis. I use the term to mean primarily the following aspects, which I discussed in more detail in the previous chapter.

First, it is the financial sector, which ballooned before our eyes, including the media and research industry servicing this segment. Second, it encompasses the vast segment of legal, management, and information services for business, including financial analysis and audit. Third, I include in the new economy the activities of management bodies of transnational corporations and attendant firms servicing these activities as outsourcers. Fourth, the new economy is represented by developers of exponentially proliferating "new products" and brands that are protected by intellectual property rights. Fifth, it also includes the segment of generously compensated advertising and marketing services, as well as the seemingly infinite number of consultants essentially acting as intermediaries on all conceivable issues. And finally, it is the retail trade and services sector that meets the needs of those employed in all of the other segments.

In contrast to the business activities characteristic of the "industrial" stage, which was marked by a strong orientation toward the end-user's needs and demands, postindustrial structure is to a large extent self-sufficient and self-serving, possessing a virtually unlimited ability to generate demand through intellectual and psychological pressure on the consumer.

This entire enormous structure, which engulfed the manufacturing sector and other related industrial structures, turned out to be localized almost exclusively in developed countries and was filled by their citizens used to high and, even more important, rising standards of consumption.

Moreover, the pluralistic system of electoral competition in these countries forced their governments to heed the demands of their citizens to do their utmost to protect their jobs, revenue sources, and standards of consumption, irrespective of the considerations of expediency or domestic and international justice. Thus the governments of developed countries expanded social security systems, while taking measures to protect jobs and incomes in the new economy through introduction of additional requirements, generating new demand for various services and the protection of intellectual property rights. Widely publicized condemnations of trade protectionism by leaders of the world's richest economies never produced measures that could affect the position of their leading financial institutions, insurance and consulting companies, law firms, media corporations, and the like, while demands to ease restrictions stemming from intellectual property rights were effectively ignored. At the same time, incomes of those employed in the "new economy" were in effect freed from regulation and were allowed to rise as fast and as high as producers of these services could engineer via the arbitrary fees they charged their clients.

Simultaneously, Western governments persistently sought to apply to developing countries the requirements and standards that generated still new demand for intellectual products of their new economy. For example, the imposition of requirements to protect the rights of owners of trademarks and other types of intellectual property and the auditing of financial statements have become standard, though sometimes implicit, means of securing constant demand for intellectual rights and products offered by core agents of postindustrial economies.

As a result of these measures taken by many nations of the developed world over the past few decades a new system emerged for dividing labor in the world economy, where developed countries derive much of their revenue via the "historical royalty": payment, directly or indirectly, through public or private distribution channels, for intellectual property. The services of Western banks, investment companies, insurers, law firms and auditors, information providers, ratings agencies, advertising and marketing firms and departments, and so on generate billions of dollars for the citizens of developed Western countries. This makes it easy for them to pay their labor at a far higher rate than is available to the average citizen of a developing country, who may have received the same education and have virtually the same talents but resides outside the boundaries of the developed Western world.

This principle also applies to the fashion industry, the information and entertainment industry, education and cultural services—each contains a vast royalty (rent) component indicative of historical circumstances and the inertia of human consciousness. A look at the background of people who constitute the political, business, and intellectual elite of most developing countries reveals that in most cases they were educated and trained in the West, if only because leading Western universities, with their centuries-long history, have status and fame that is unattainable for Third World educational establishments. Rich and famous people from non-Western countries send and will continue to send their children to Eton, Oxford and Cambridge, MIT and West Point, Chicago and Bologna.

For the same reason the Italian fashion industry, British and U.S. pop music, Hollywood cinema, and U.S. television will not in the immediate future face serious competition from similar industries in the non-Western world. We cannot take seriously the argument that U.S. and European companies dominate these sectors strictly via better productivity (the very concept of productivity in the services sector raises many questions and gives too few answers) or because of the financial and human resources they have accumulated. It is evident that their domination is supported as well by the subordination of consumer behavior to historical stereotypes reinforced by daily advertising, as well as by inertia of human behavioral and cultural patterns.[3] The result is that competition in many key markets (when ranked by sales volume) of intellectual and cultural products is subject to fairly rigid constraints permitting oligopolies to include in their product prices a fee for historical and organizational components that they simply own as heirs, at no perceivable cost.

In other words, the growing "royalty" component in the price of manufactured and exported products (including services and sale of intellectual property, in both explicit and implicit forms) enables producers of such products to receive more and more revenue that does not reflect direct costs, and to create economic niches (like business-related ratings, rankings, high-level business consulting, auditing, and the like) that are essentially unavailable to or even hidden from outsiders. These niches have always been the domain of wealthy countries with a history of putting self-interest first, thereby displaying Realeconomik characteristics. The niches and associated revenue are protected by leveraging government support, for example, through the institution of intellectual property rights and the introduction of stringent defenses, including requirements that foreign countries comply with restrictions and preferences arising from these rights. Additional restrictions involve the promotion in foreign countries of norms and standards that have been adapted to serve the interests of the producers of the original goods and services.[4]

This is a key point whenever we try to evaluate the existing system of international relations and prospects for its future evolution. While essential for understanding the motives underlying actions of the political class in many countries of the former Third World, this point has never been the focus of public discussion or even earnest scholarly analysis. This book is intended, in part, to address that deficiency.

Always Lagging Behind

It is easy to see also the other side to this coin—the intentional or involuntary allocation of the invariable role of loser to the part of the world that by force of circumstance or history has been deprived of the chance to develop or gain control over intangible assets, which not only bring hefty royalties to their owners but also give them a possibility to control internationally the "rules of the game."[5] Over the past two centuries this unfortunate part of the world constantly has been in the position of an athlete ordered by the event organizers to offer a head start to its opponents. Moreover, in this competition, which basically involves grabbing a larger proportion of global wealth, the head start is constantly granted to the richer participants, to the detriment of poorer players.

As a result, it is becoming harder and harder to imagine that the gap separating the richest economies from the countries lagging behind in economic development will ever be overcome. This does not mean that it is impossible for one or two countries to achieve such a historic leap. But such a possibility exists only in isolated cases, not as a common phenomenon, and even such an exception is becoming ever less likely.

Only a hundred years ago every nation had a realistic chance to compete, and the result was not clearly predetermined. If a country had a reasonably structured economic life owing to the diligence, labor, talent, and education of its population, that country could improve materially its international ranking in terms of wealth and economic might. Admittedly, a significant role was played by natural factors—the favorable environmental and climatic conditions and guaranteed access to natural resources (often attained primarily by military and administrative control in the absence of a developed global commodity market)—which constituted an important and indispensable condition for successful economic growth.

At the time, past achievements did not play the key role in determining the outcome of the competitive struggle. The United States, many less-developed countries in the Old World, and Australia all illustrate vividly that an initial state of poverty during incipient capitalism did not impede accelerated development and an increase in the average level of consumption and production to extremely high rates for that era. (Admittedly, at that time the gap between poor and relatively prosperous countries was not as wide as nowadays, and could be overcome within the life span of just one generation, provided conditions were set for realizing entrepreneurial talents and ambitions of most gifted, energetic, and success-oriented people in a given country.)

In the current environment, the world seems permanently divided into countries that are rich or poor, strong or weak, making great bounds forward or lagging far behind.

As I have argued, assertions by some countries that they are progressing toward the ranks of developed nations have yet to be proved, and rising consumption in a narrow stratum benefiting from increased exports is not sufficient to support such claims. But even if we assume that there will be one or two exceptions, they do not change the general rule: no visible signs point to the eradication of the existing assignment of roles in the world economy that enforce radically different levels of income and consumption among countries. This stratification is all the more intractable because countries are assigned their roles with respect not only to producing and trading goods and services but to setting the relevant rules and standards.[6]

It is true that anywhere on the globe you can accumulate cash or borrow, set up competitive production facilities, and make good-quality, inexpensive goods. However, the income per employee will invariably be less than the income to be obtained by the owner of the intellectual and organizational resource that makes it possible not only to satisfy consumer demands but also to shape that demand to a large extent. And while owners in the "old" economy (industrial and even postindustrial) can achieve impressive results in terms of individual wealth, the income levels and opportunities available to workers in those sectors are inferior to those of the people who create new demand and add new links to production chains, whose costs will invariably be included in the price and covered by end consumers, thereby guaranteeing a high rate of return for their activities.[7]

Production capabilities to satisfy basic human needs are progressing in poor countries as well, but the gap between the developed and so-called developing world is not narrowing. Moreover, the very term *developing,* which for the sake of political correctness has replaced the expression *underdeveloped,* does not change the sad fact that these countries are as likely to join the ranks of developed countries as a peasant boy from a backwater is to head British Petroleum or Gazprom. The global distribution of economic influence in, say, the past fifty years has changed immaterially at best, and over the past fifteen years the world's "club of the wealthy" has had virtually no new members. Even a wish list of the "developing" countries that have even a slight chance of leaving that group and becoming "developed" within the next thirty years would include at best a dozen out of more than one hundred developing economies.[8] And few of them will be able to leverage this opportunity. In other words, the term *developing* is accurate only in the sense that the economic situation in these countries is not static, that there is in fact some development, even progress. However, it would be a mistake to assume that this progress will ultimately result in the transition of these countries to the group of developed countries. With some minor exceptions, second- and third-tier countries will without doubt retain their current status for the foreseeable future, remaining forever part of the "developing world."

However, the key issue here is perhaps not that the opportunities for less fortunate countries to bridge the gap have contracted perceptibly because of natural processes. Hard as they might try to adjust to international market demands, they will always lose out to the countries generating demand. The key issue is the change in perception: bridging the gap, even in a distant future, is no longer considered an indispensable objective for the sustainable growth of the global capitalist economy.

That brings us again to the underlying moral dimension to an apparently purely economic situation, using Realeconomik as a tool to view things from a different perspective. It is evident that the aforementioned U-turn in relations between the developed world and remaining countries could be partly attributed to the weakened moral constraints in the world of modern capitalism. On the other hand, this turnaround in the definition of the existing international gaps, which came to be seen as an unchangeable reality, in turn contributed to greater general cynicism with respect to the "rules of the game," not only in international trade and investment relations but in international politics as well.

This assignment of roles within the world capitalist economy has to a large extent rendered meaningless a moral approach to relations between developed and developing countries. Why bother trying to build a system of international measures to facilitate economic growth in the poorer countries if the nature of that growth is determined by the new allocation of roles in the global economy? The promotion of economic growth and investments is reduced to the concern of national governments, and the "north-south" dialogue within international organizations and various forums resembles more and more a form of horse trading. Developed countries demand increased protection for the rights of their investors and a clampdown on intellectual piracy, whereas the developing countries (or to be more precise the countries able and willing to play by the new rules) seek more access to loans from international organizations and more direct aid from Western governments.

It is possible that China could play a special role here: due to the size of the country's population, the influential role played by its government (which essentially rented out the country's people and territory to global business three decades ago), and its extraordinary financial capacities, China is demanding access to attractive forms of businesses through participation in capital or the acquisition of corporations operating in the most developed countries. Indeed, in its drive for more acquisitions China recently has been encountering more and more resistance from Western political elites and governments, though this resistance has less to do with principles than with negotiation of self-interests and areas of mutual concern. What is portrayed sometimes as issues of ideals and principle (like the recent row over political censorship of the Chinese Internet) is more often than not stubborn horse trading between elites for control over promising or critical spheres of business activity.

Of course, such an approach can have an inverse impact, as has been seen in China. The rise in pragmatism in relations between North and South over recent decades has undoubtedly contributed to the virtual abandonment of moral values in the actions of some Western governments and of global business and political elites since the end of the Cold War. The result is a reduction of international relations to a cynical zero-sum game in which the principles of Realpolitik (ruthlessness, power politics, force, and bluff of force) have supplanted the ideals of universal progress that characterized mainstream political and economic thought in the twentieth century.

A digression will buttress this point. Serious attempts at bringing morality into international politics were first made earlier in the twentieth century, when statesmen on the winning side in World War I tried to lay the foundation for a more fair international order. Chief among these attempts was the creation of the League of Nations, embodying the concept of an alliance of democratic nations based on common values, and an appeal to people's democratic instincts. There was reason to hope that historical and social progress was starting to reshape the whole system of international relations, infusing it with a long-term vision of an international order based on principles rather than narrowly understood national interests.

After the interruption of World War II, these aims regained momentum. Competition among alternative systems, particularly between Western capitalism and the Soviet Union's version of communism, made elites of most Western countries adhere to some simple principles of a fair world order. These principles have been openly proclaimed and largely adhered to: respect for human rights, economic and political freedom in international relations, help for the needy and facilitation of economic development, protection of Western economic systems against undue interference or intrusion from states with corporate systems of government. But the principles once proclaimed and upheld have clearly been revised, or have come to be ignored. Consider the readiness of Western governments to accept and even solicit investment from countries whose economies are controlled by "strong leaders or by corporate states"—China, for example. This is still another manifestation of the decline in public discipline and moral constraint in the wake of modern capitalism's victory in the Cold War. Once the sense of military danger vanished, all other dangers—including the danger that the values underlying capitalist systems and serving as a prerequisite for an efficient functioning of economic market mechanisms were in decline—seemed to become unworthy of serious attention. Neither the American nor the European economy is in imminent danger from the growing trend toward state-controlled companies and sovereign funds managed by people loyal to an ideological or corporate government, be it

China or an Arab monarchy. Nevertheless, this trend can have a substantial long-term influence on the value-based attitudes in business communities and in the Western economy as a whole.

The same is true of the seemingly insurmountable and largely antagonistic gap between rich countries and their poor counterparts. The ever-widening abyss between one-third of the population and the remaining two-thirds in terms of income, education, health, safety, living standards, and longevity will, together with the environment, become a critical issue in the twenty-first century.

International politics over the past fifteen years has amply demonstrated these trends. However, before discussing this issue, I would like to say a few words about another relevant phenomenon confronted by global capitalism over the past twenty years: the collapse of the Soviet Union and the Soviet economic system that it embodied.

Breakup of the USSR and Post-Soviet Transformation: Short-Term Interest Versus Moral Principles

The breakup of the Soviet Union is considered by some to be a major victory and by others as the greatest geopolitical disaster of the second half of the twentieth century. It signaled the end of a major world-wide experiment: an attempt to create a historically sustainable economic social model capable of progressive development and based on principles other than modern capitalism, including material restrictions on individual private property, rejection of the market as the main regulator of use of economic resources, and central planning as the main instrument for structuring business.

Although you will still find some people, at least in Russia, who claim that the collapse of the USSR was not attributable to the inadequacy and inefficiency of the Soviet economic system, it remains true that the economic system created by the Soviet Union also collapsed at the same time. Now that system is represented globally only in tiny enclaves in self-insulated countries (for instance, Cuba or North Korea). The national economies emerging in the 1990s from the carcass of the Soviet economy naturally bear the imprint of their Soviet past. In general, however, the economic system in former Soviet countries resembles its predecessor in the USSR far less than it does the economic systems of countries with similar economic, natural, and cultural backgrounds that never experienced the Soviet version of socialism. Although the underlying mechanisms functioning in the Russian economy today differ from corresponding mechanisms in the economies of the United States or Britain, say, they are no less "capitalist" than similar mechanisms in Indonesia or Brazil, or in Italy or Japan before World War II. Countries of the former USSR can be classified as a separate group within the global economy only for limited academic purposes. Furthermore, all economic or philosophical talk, whether positive or negative, about "Russia's special path" represents nothing more than speculation and populism ingrained either in Russian nationalism or in a nationalistic or ideological rejection of Russia.[9]

I have sought to describe in detail the specifics of Russian capitalism in works such as *Peripheral Capitalism* and *Russia's Prospects*. Against the backdrop of my analysis of the specifics of Russia's current economic system, I tried to convey the idea that we are dealing with capitalism and its basic characteristics, like private property and the market logic of business behavior, but with an underdeveloped civil society, weak and shaky government institutions, and strong dependence on the world capitalist economy. Accordingly, Russia at the end of the previous century and the start of the current one, despite all the differences in the conditions it faced at various periods of its post-Soviet history, suffered simultaneously from the inadequate development of capitalism, including numerous flaws that it inherited from its precapitalist past, and from attempts to introduce it in the forms totally unsuited to Russia's condition. Certain aspects of the capitalist economic system were introduced that were appropriate for a completely different stage: the stage of postindustrial capitalism, with forms assuming an all-encompassing nature completely disassociated from their original intent or meaning. As a result, the country was engulfed in an inexplicable and phantasmagorical situation, in which institutions and forms borrowed from Western postindustrial "financial capitalism" coexisted with almost medieval relations within the government bureaucracy and between that bureaucracy and the society at large.

For example, a stock market was set up in Russia—perhaps not the most sophisticated of its kind, but fairly complete in form, diversified and supported by adequate technical infrastructure. However, it emerged in a country without a tradition of large-scale private property, and it offered virtually no guarantees for rights of either minority or controlling shareholders of corporations. The judicial system and commercial arbitration in Russia may have assumed all the forms appropriate in a capitalist society, but intrinsically they constituted nothing but an instrument for defending (at best, coordinating) the interests of politically influential people and groups. At the same time, the office of the public prosecutor and investigative authorities, charged with supervising the legality of the actions of commercial entities, were far less adept at exercising their duties than had been the analogous authorities near the end of the Soviet era. Meanwhile, the business community in Russia today is a peculiar social group, whose status, interests, and identity are vague and resist articulate or consistent description.

Joint Venture

The economic system of modern Russia is in general a separate and extremely complex matter. Bearing in mind the contradictory and multidimensional nature of the interdependent economic relations that coexist in a single system in a way that is not always rationally explicable, it is impossible to provide a coherent picture of that system in several sentences. However, it is important to remember that the present economic system of Russia didn't appear by chance. Nor could the system have been imposed by the outside world. But neither can it be understood as a purely Russian national phenomenon that evolved with no outside influence or interference. It was instead erected on a foundation left by the former USSR, radically reengineered by post-Soviet Russia with substantial input from the outside world, primarily the West as a special geopolitical reality. To a certain extent Russia today, with all its contradictions, failures, and complex attitudes toward the outside world, is the product of the collective creativity of late-Soviet elites who reached the pinnacle of power at the time of the collapse of the Soviet Union, and of the Western governments, which by virtue of their position and ability to influence events in the global economy bear responsibility for all major economic developments in the world.

Both theoretically and practically it is the moral prerogative of the Western governments to take responsibility for the future of the world economy, including the economies of non-Western nations. I see this prerogative as a natural product of their great capabilities, which carry with them corresponding moral duty and responsibility.

In fact, the history and circumstances of the post-Soviet transformation of Russia make it is clear that the West played an important role in this process, with all the contradictory consequences. The process was fundamentally tied to domestic factors and was driven by forces unrelated to either Western governments or nongovernmental institutions. Nevertheless, the evolution of this process depended to a large extent on the reactions of the West to these developments, on its choice of people to converse with, and on the manner in which it waged this dialogue.[10]

Formally, the West reacted to events in Russia with support for democratic forces, support for the country's transition from totalitarianism to democracy. At the same time, however, the concept of democracy is extremely broad and can take on very different content depending on the initial attitude and interests of the speaker. We will not consider here the initial definition of democracy as "power of the people." From the very beginning in 1991 this definition was recognized as a pure abstraction and cast aside. One can find numerous different definitions of democracy, but the popular understanding propagated by some politically minded intellectuals is too narrow in a country lacking fundamental democratic culture. It privileges procedures (in particular, the holding of elections) and the regulation of processes to coordinate the interests of different groups. Regimes considered absolutely undemocratic in the West can draft state procedures that stand up against the best examples of such regulations adopted in the democratic world. These procedures can serve as the subject of wide-ranging debates, including the establishment of appropriate commissions and piles of bureaucratic work—as was the case, for example, before the adoption of the Soviet Constitution. Moreover, the regulations can be followed to the letter in these regimes. After all, Hitler was an elected leader, and his election in 1933 took place in strict accordance with the law and was never challenged on legal ground.

It is similarly unproductive to define democracy on the basis of the principles of the electivity and accountability of officials and a separation of executive, legislative, and judicial branches and the like. The declaration of these principles may reflect a specific set of ideals, and in that sense may be juxtaposed against another set of principles (for example, the unity and indivisibility of power). But the way these principles are formally manifested may reveal a state structure that privileges very different types of power relations and management of society.

In short, democracy should be understood to mean primarily the distribution of power among various groups of influence and political competition based on the subordination of all participants to rules established under the rule of law, culminating in elections as a mechanism for arbitration between groups competing for power. From the outset of its post-

Soviet history, modern Russia has taken only the most hesitant and limited steps along this path, stopping or even turning backward when confronted by the possibility of genuine replacement of the ruling team. No changes have occurred at the top of the state pyramid since the emergence of the "new democratic Russia." The regime has merely reproduced itself by re-placing members of the team at its own discretion; general elections have been held as, at best, an idiosyncratic poll of public opinion (which was in turn formed by the regime), with no binding consequences. Freedom has been permitted in the media only to the extent that it could not have seri-ous political consequences or create any threat of regime change.

Initially there were regional instances of one influential group forcibly replacing another in local elections, although no one could guarantee that the organizers and supervisors of the elections had abided by the written rules. However, by the start of the twenty-first century, even regional poli-tics was under the effective control of the top of the government hierar-chy, which effectively ruled out the holding of unpredictable elections.

The extent of the influence of such a system over economic relations, especially property issues, is a special consideration.[11] I have tried to pro-vide an answer in some of my works,[12] showing that the political system existing in post-Soviet Russia is characterized by permanent authoritarian power, a bloated state bureaucracy, and a subordinate role played by law in the regulation of economic life. The system has one main attribute: the actual relations of ownership and management of economic assets, their expropriation, and so on, are regulated less by formal legal norms (irre-spective of whether they are satisfactory or not) than by force, including covert unofficial power. As such power is protean, its influence over time is uncertain. Thus private ownership of large assets in Russia is widely be-lieved to be conditional, temporary, and unaccompanied by recognition of the formal owner's right to full and unconditional disposal of such assets or products produced with them. This applies to the entire post-Soviet pe-riod and not only, as has been claimed by many liberal-minded politicians and political scholars, to the past few years, when democracy and legality were dramatically curtailed. (The latter assertion is based on the tacit assump-tion that before 2002–2003 Russia was, barring a few minor mishaps, a law-based democratic country or was at least moving in that direction.) It is true that a number of institutions and procedures traditionally interpreted as democratic were in fact dismantled after 2003. However, the substance of relations between the regime and the groups of successful and influential people in the country, including as applied to control of major property, remained in general unchanged throughout the period since 1991.

"Democratic Friends"

Furthermore, the past ten years in Russia have not brought the country any closer to a competitive political system and represent not a turning point but rather a continuation of trends dating back to the 1990s. I wrote about these trends in *Demodernization* before Putin's so-called rejection of the democratic path of development. At that time I tried to convey that in the 1990s an irreplaceable stratum of the uppermost bureaucracy had formed in Russia and that both the political system and business lived by rules that were independent of formal political and legal institutions. At the time, this situation was accepted by a significant number of people in the Russian elite, including some who started to voice their concerns about the dangers and the futility of the system only several years later.

Meanwhile, Western governments and many Western intellectuals calmly observed the development of the political and economic system in post-Soviet Russia and asserted that there was nothing threatening about the process as long as the stratum of the uppermost bureaucracy was ready to cooperate with the West, primarily with the United States, on priority issues. Essentially, the criterion for democracy in Russia at that time could be reduced to a simple, circular formula: democracy exists when "democrats" are in power. And "democrats" are the people who consider us to be their friends and whom we accordingly treat as our friends. The more they are our friends, the more they are "democrats." (Incidentally, this simplistic formula applies not only to Russia but to other countries of the former Soviet Union, the former Yugoslavia, and several other nations. It was widely implemented and continues to be applied to the entire post-communist world.)

However simplistic, this criterion was at least applied cautiously and flexibly, with due consideration for reality. Thus in cases when the West's "democratic friends" were obviously marginal to the political elite and had no chance of influencing Russia's policies, they were effectively ignored. At the same time, anyone opposed to the regime who seemed capable of rising in influence was cautiously embraced.[13] On the other hand, some members of the ruling bureaucratic team were accorded maximum support as long as they displayed a benevolent attitude to the West and were ready, in exchange for support, to consider the specific interests of specific countries in Russian politics. As a result, the role of "chief democrats" and forces incarnating Russia's rosy future in the West's public opinion was assigned to so-called liberals (mostly former Komsomol and Communist Party functionaries) from Yeltsin's team, who seemed fairly close to the West ideologically and capable of exerting substantial influence on Russian foreign policy. According to the predominant view of post-Soviet Russia, it was in the interests of the West to support, on the one hand, the influential people in Russia who appeared most inclined to listen to the opinion of the West, and, on the other hand, the most influential people among those promising the West their friendship.[14]

Friendship in general, and in politics in particular, rarely comes for free. Sometimes it can even cost money. But no one likes to spend money. And it turned out that financial aid to Russia, which the liberal wing of Yeltsin's team was counting on, was modest. It looks especially modest when set against the scale of the victory of the West in the Cold War and the challenge of transforming a vast totalitarian economy into a Western-model free-market system. In any case, compared with the sums handed out today in Western countries to try to tame the Great Recession, the financial aid provided to Russia at the time by international financial institutions appears minuscule. Moreover, a significant proportion of this aid went to foreign consultants or paid for training programs of dubious value.

Consequently, the West paid for friendship primarily with what appeared to be the cheapest option: moral support for the dubious domestic politics of the Russian leadership, which at the time was demonstrating wondrous flexibility in avoiding moral restraint.[15] If it were a question only of individual cases of corruption, one might have been able to justify closing one's eyes in the name of the great cause. Tragically, the Russian government at the time, while relatively clean in terms of personal enrichment, was totally indifferent to the interests of the public. As a result, the government flouted any notion that there are universally held moral values other than personal wealth, that values respected and supported by the state dictate that citizens receive adequate reward for honest labor, thrift, compliance with the law, respect for the interests of other people, and public service.

The leadership in those days did everything possible to convince the public that the opposite was true through its actions and even more so through inaction. Several years of rampant inflation, measured in hundreds and thousands of percentage points, constituted a brutal punishment for the workforce trying to save money. Honest officials and policemen, doctors, and teachers had to live on the edge. Their salaries were not indexed adequately, and in many cases they were not paid at all for months at a time because of an alleged shortfall in state revenues. Law and order appeared beyond repair: enforcement agencies survived on unofficial services for those who could pay, including criminals, instead of a bankrupt state budget. Tax collection was haphazard, and state property was doled out almost for free to the smoothest operators to "expedite the creation of a broad stratum of property owners." State television and other media lionized the people who had suddenly grown rich in the lawless chaos as "effective managers," calling on all the poor—workers, peasants, honest civil servants, engineers, scientists and scholars, policemen, doctors, and teachers—"to learn how to make money" and "set up their own small businesses." Such developments as the sudden rise in mortality from stress, mental illness, alcoholism, and the lack of access for the poor to basic medical aid were either ignored or attributed to the onerous legacy of the Soviet period.[16] Meanwhile, the people gazing on from the Kremlin and ministerial offices promoted themselves (and continue to do so) as heroes who had saved the country from famine, economic collapse, civil war, and a return of the Communist regime.[17]

In my opinion, however, civil war did not break out in Russia (although there were manifest signs that it was starting in 1993) because of a genuine belief in the need for a clean break from Soviet life. People understood the need for reforms and believed that they would change their lives and the lives of their children for the better. This belief was betrayed, and a group of cynical individuals came to power, riding on the shoulders of millions of people who had dreamed of dismantling the Soviet system in Russia. These individuals applied Bolshevik methods based on the principle that power justifies everything and the end justifies the means. That is why the disillusionment and apathy after 2000 were so profound. The absolute majority of the population supported then-president Vladimir Putin's authoritarian regime and essentially rejected almost all the democratic forms stipulated by the constitution.

Short-Term Gain and Strategic Dead End

It was easy, though, to perceive the reality of the situation. Take, for example, Jeffrey Sachs, who had initially sincerely sympathized with the "young liberals" and was a leading proponent of "shock therapy" at the time. He subsequently said: "The Russian reform process was a debacle. I stayed for two years [1992–1993], but then got fed up with both the 'West,' which was not helping Russia properly, and Russia, which was not reforming properly. After 1993, especially 1995 and 1996, the corruption really exploded. I watched sadly from the sidelines. Alas, the U.S. Administration did little to try to slow the corruption. It basically just looked away. It was the corruption in the mid-1990s, in the 'oil for shares' deals, that created many of the 'oligarchs' who are at the center of controversy today."[18]

After 1991 the U.S. and European administrations conducted themselves with the conviction that internationally, Russia was a country of limited significance with a specific leader-oriented mentality. So they focused on relationship building with the person whom they thought to be an effective national leader, abandoning policies in the process. Not only did they let themselves tolerate a gap between proclaimed democratic principles and actual actions by Russian authorities, they also sent a clear message to Russian top authorities that public attitudes in the West could be properly shaped or ignored provided the top Russian leader remained receptive to practical interests and concerns of the West—for example, the liquidation of the military and political threat that the Soviet Union had represented. No matter what former officials, or their advisers, who dealt with Russia after the demise of the Soviet Union may say to the contrary, this is exactly the stance that they took first with Yeltsin and then with Putin, putting interests ahead of principles and short-term political gains at home ahead of a longer perspective of a more just and safer international order.

It isn't clear whether this stance was taken out of mere convenience or whether there was a true conviction of the successive White House administrations of Presidents Clinton and Bush that it was the only way of doing business with Russia. Perhaps it was a combination of the two, as well as some other factors, like cultural misunderstandings or sincere but convenient hope that with time Russian leaders would learn all the merits of being true friends of the West. Irrespective of the underlying motives, the approach sent a clear message: if we strike a deal, everyone else will have to swallow it in the end.

At times it seemed to work to everybody's satisfaction. It worked with Yeltsin and his circle, which was often referred to as the Family. It worked even more with Putin of the early 2000s, hardening his instinctive disregard for the force of public opinion and his conviction that it was not "principles" but the will of strong leaders that matter in politics, both international and domestic. But later developments revealed this approach to be disastrous. As in economics, the attempt to make rapid and easy gains requires closing your eyes to the growth of long-term, systemic risks—one of the main guiding principles of Realeconomik. Endorsement of chaotic, semicriminal, but rapid privatization in Russia in the 1990s reduced the short-term risk of a public return to the power of the people with views and conceptions of a profoundly Soviet nature. However, in the long term it increased the likelihood that a major nuclear power would switch to a development path leading to a dead end, with all the concomitant risks and consequences for the rest of the world.

Was there a realistic alternative? Could a different position in the West at the time have facilitated the development of the Russian political and economic system along a different path? I believe so. At the start of the reforms in 1990–1991, the situation was flexible. The implementation of a well-planned, professional, and politically honest approach, like the Marshall Plan in Europe after World War II, could have had an extremely positive impact.[19] I don't know whether such an approach would have been decisive, but the adoption of a more moral position by the West could have influenced the mindset inside the country, depriving some forces of ideological trump cards and strengthening other forces characterized by healthier ideas and morals. Such a position would not have required costly aid programs or any significant sacrifices by Western taxpayers. The more important gesture would have been calling things by their proper names, refusing to endorse cynical policies of Russian "democratic" leadership or to tolerate their illegal and immoral profiteering at the expense of public funds and national resources.

Moreover, various spheres of activity of people and society are interrelated and influence one another, and if the negative impact of the convenient position that was adopted by the West toward Russia and other countries of the former Soviet Union may be subject to debate, the adverse influences of this position on the ethical climate in Western countries themselves was manifest.

You cannot build a business on deceit and at the same time expect scrupulous honesty and decency from your employees.[20] You cannot defend human rights in one country and ignore them with contempt in another. You cannot support a cynical and immoral policy in other countries without weakening the moral compass in your own country. It might be impossible to support this statement with data (although it would probably not be difficult to build an econometric model on the influence of increased incidences of fraud or bribery on GDP growth rates, showing both direct and inverse dependencies). But I am convinced that this factor—the short-sighted, Realeconomik belief that the transformation of the post-Soviet space is important only to remove direct threats to security and prosperity, and that the social climate in this space can be left to Providence—is one of the causes of the contemporary crisis in "financial capitalism." If we are to consider morality in international politics and the link to the problems of modern capitalism, it is obvious that the position adopted by the West with respect to post-Soviet transformation is only one such episode. But it shows vividly that unresolved problems in international relations influenced the general moral climate in developed countries, which in its turn contributed to the unexplainable tolerance toward dangerous and risky actions by economic agents, actions that otherwise could have been identified and addressed in a timely fashion.

International Politics in 1990–2008: Rejection of Global Political Philosophy for a Practical Solution to Local Problems by Using Economic Levers and Force

Major decisions in international relations taken in disregard of moral values are not confined to the issues raised by the dangerous gaps between the more affluent and less fortunate nations or by transformation of former communist economies.

After the Soviet and then the Russian leadership abandoned the idea of global confrontation with the developed world, which implied the end to forty years of the Cold War, many people—myself included—came away with the hope that a new era was about to begin. Confrontation would be consigned to the past, and it would be possible to coordinate the interests of major world powers in the name of general development and the improvement of living standards throughout the world. When I worked in 1990–1991 on the Soviet-American project called the Grand Bargain I felt that many people shared these hopes.[21]

More than twenty years later these hopes have failed to reach fruition. Over the past two decades, international politics have failed to solve a single regional problem, let alone issues in the world order. This applies to the situations in Iraq, Afghanistan, Bosnia, Somalia, Pakistan, Kashmir, Sri

Lanka, the Philippines, and especially the Middle East, to the status of Taiwan and Kosovo, the situation with the Kurds in Turkey, territorial disputes in the post-Soviet space—the list is long. The issue of nonproliferation of nuclear weapons has not been solved, and relations with Iran and North Korea remain unstable. The international community has been utterly impotent in its actions in Rwanda and Srebrenica. Diplomatic and political efforts have in virtually every case failed to improve the situation; each specific example is unique, but the situations all remain inauspicious and potentially explosive.

The ability of the United States and Europe to project their power is weakening. This is demonstrated by long-term trends in voting in key U.N. agencies. The policies of the West in such a wide range of crisis regions—from Georgia to Zimbabwe, from Burma (Myanmar) and the Balkans to Kosovo and Darfur, to the ongoing struggle to secure approval of global measures against Iran's nuclear ambitions—all end up in fiasco. Ten years ago, 72 percent of U.N. member nations supported Europe's policies in human rights; by 2009 this figure had fallen to 48 percent. An even greater decline is perceptible in the case of support for U.S. positions, from 77 percent to 30 percent. Long-standing disputes between Russia and the European Union and the United States have now come to the fore. Of course, it is always possible to find someone to blame for these failures and defeats, to look for underhanded practices of enemies of the "Western world," especially as resistance grows to the efforts of the United States and Europe. But a more rational assessment would lead to a startling admission: the quality of the foreign policy of Western countries has deteriorated perceptibly over the past twenty years.

Above all, this is true of the United States, whose policies have to a large extent defined the world throughout the postwar era. After the end of the Cold War, the United States was the last "superpower" in the world. Has America used this immense responsibility effectively?

Many in America misunderstood its victory in the Cold War and perceived the start of the new century as "the end of history." This meant that the United States started to implement policies internationally with the assumption that the whole world would now follow the path of American-style democracy, more or less in accordance with the old army principle: "If you don't know how, we'll teach you; if you don't want to, we'll make you."

In reality, however, the end of the age of confrontation freed most countries to declare their cultural and religious diversity and transform their cultural aspirations into political reality. Until then such diversity had existed, but it had been subsumed by membership in one or another bloc. The cumulative population of all Western countries amounts to some 700 million, or about 10 percent of the planet's population. The remaining 90 percent, until now primarily an object of world history, is now starting to play a leading role.

The modern world is extremely diverse in many respects, not only in terms of wealth distribution and prosperity levels. Its diversity manifests itself also in the organization of society and prevailing values and traditions. Moreover, the differences of organization of society cannot be reduced to a predetermined historical sequence of development. It would be a grave error to assume that all countries are following the same path but have merely reached different stages on this route—that countries in Africa or the Middle East one hundred or two hundred years from now will have social and economic structures that match the current organization of life in western Europe or the United States. The concept of a single future for all countries and peoples is the greatest myth of the twentieth century, embraced by both the Marxists and their opponents in the Cold War. Today, early in the twenty-first century, the world is no more united or homogeneous than it was a century or two ago, and you don't have to be a great prophet to assert confidently that the world will be just as heterogeneous a century from now.

However the West, and primarily the United States, proceeds in its policies from the opposite thesis. The mission to civilize is prevalent in the arguments used to defend the actions of the United States and its allies in Iraq and Afghanistan. The thesis also appears in the most varied areas of foreign policy: stances toward different parts of the post-Soviet space; the attempts to transform NATO from a military union into a political tool; the growing anti-Islamic tilt; the increasingly obvious attempts to present international problems in black and white, as a universal battle between good and evil, good and bad guys.

This perspective appears all the more incongruous at a time when the "forces of good" have little obvious military advantage: America's might is still measured by the parameters of the twentieth century. Aircraft carriers and heavy bombers were ideal to contain the Soviet bloc, but the threats in the twenty-first century are of a different order. Other measures are required to combat terrorism, various misanthropic religions and ideologies, nationalism, climatic cataclysms, the proliferation of nuclear weapons, and energy imbalances. Above all, the broadest cooperation is required, with all parties open to dialogue. This necessitates the acceptance of different opinions, and the elaboration of general solutions, not a condescending pat on the shoulder. The logic of intimidating inconvenient or unaccommodating countries via hostility and isolation, transforming their neighbors into a "quasi-frontline zone" or inviting them to participate in ruinous military expeditions—if it bore any legitimacy to begin with—is long since out of date.

The Quality of Political Thought

The foreign policy of the United States and Europe was far from ideal after the end of the Cold War, but this cannot be attributed to a lack of information or a misunderstanding of objective laws of world development. Rather, it is connected to the same factors underlying the Great Recession: the predominance of politicians who preferred the political pragmatism of Realpolitik to the politics of principles and humanitarian values.

By pragmatism, I do not mean simply practicality in pursuit of socially significant positive goals. Pragmatism, when manifested in the search for realistic ways to achieve lofty social goals, is not only justified but moral. Flexibility has never been a sign of weakness; on the contrary, inflexibility often indicates weakness of intellect. Rather, I am talking about pragmatism of a different kind—the cynical attitude of a person devoid of higher goals, ideals, and principles, who selects the simplest and easiest path to personal gain. For a politician, there is always an easy way: instead of trying to convince voters and leaders of the rightness and benefits of a proposed program, he can simply go with the general flow. Worse, he can seek to elevate himself by playing up to the base side of human nature—holding others in contempt or oppressing their will, reflexively rejecting anything new or difficult to understand, grasping after the prosperity and power of others, and so on. If the general level of moral standards in a society is in decline, the temptation to follow such a path increases exponentially. In such circumstances, following a policy based on force instead of dialogue and coexistence seems the natural choice.

We have examined the moral frustration of a public compelled to adapt to the postmodern reality of "financial capitalism," where the real result of honest labor loses its value compared with the fortunes arising from thin air and obtained with the support and protection of the state. Against this backdrop, unprincipled experts and ignorant politicians may find irresistible the temptation to exploit the notion of a "conflict of civilizations," of a struggle with the "enemies of freedom" abroad. Hence the mixture of arrogance and blindness exhibited by influential political players, with their depressing ability to finesse the freedoms of civil society, which has in turn displayed in recent years a disturbing readiness to forgo human rights for the sake of security.

The reverse side of public hubris and arrogance is tacit private cynicism —the readiness to overlook inconvenient facts, lies, torture in secret prisons, and the financial crimes of "our" politicians. The interrelation of public and private produces the "trade and buy politics," underlying this morality, based on oil and gas flows, opaque deals, and corporate interests.

The deterioration of the moral atmosphere of international politics is accompanied by a decline in the responsibility of the news media around the world, which are simply being transformed into propaganda machines. Moreover, glamour and show business have, with the help of television, made politics less professional and even more isolated from public interest.

It is already possible to state with confidence that the efforts of the so-called G-20 have had little impact on the current situation in the global economy. This is in part attributable to the fact that the leaders meeting for crisis discussions cannot sincerely discuss the real reasons of the Great Recession. They cannot respond to such questions as the following, for example: Why is it wrong to disseminate substandard securities if it was all right to bamboozle international public opinion about the existence of weapons of mass destruction and on this basis start a war? Why is it acceptable for the most democratic country in the world to engage in torture, but wrong to issue bad loans? If they were to discuss such issues, they would need to talk not only about greedy bankers but also about their own role, about the Western political system as a whole, about the dramatic degeneration in the quality of politics, and about the fact that big business, primarily the financial sector, has merged with and to an extent come to dominate politics over the past few decades.

It is proving difficult and expensive to overcome the crisis because politicians are reluctant to implement the necessary mass bankruptcies. The scale is too large. The social consequences would be catastrophic. In addition, if the politicians go in this direction, business, which is boxed into a corner, may ask the political establishment: who set an example of cynicism and hypocrisy? Who turned world politics into an international arena for trading in principles? Who demonstrated irresponsible overconfidence? Who failed to understand the meaning of the end of the Cold War? And so on and so forth. As a result, politicians decided to pay instead of answering questions. And even when enormous bailouts ostensibly improved the situation, it remained essentially the same, and the extremely dangerous process we witnessed continued: modern politics and economics became increasingly inadequate to the realities of the new century.

The essential problem remains: to address the disease—the economic crisis—merely by splashing more and more money over it without going into the roots and looking for ultimate causes merely relieves the symptoms, leaving the causes intact. Investors and all the other participants in the global economic game could see that something was missing and that confidence was not returning to the market. The real recovery from the crisis was being postponed.

5

The Crisis in Russia Is a Different Matter

In view of my personal experience as someone directly involved in Russian realities, who had an opportunity both to participate in them and observe developments from within, I now turn, in view of everything I have written on the Great Recession of the early twenty-first century, to my impression of how it affects Russia.

The Russian economic system not only is a reflection of the cultural and historical development of the country and the reform of the Soviet economy; it also developed to a great extent out of the powerful influence of modern trends in the Western economy. Indeed, the rebirth of capitalism in Russia in the 1990s has become a sort of a mirror reflecting recent developments in mainstream capitalism. More than seventy years of "anticapitalism" under communist rule have destroyed the historical basis on which contemporary capitalism evolved in Europe and the United States, the foundation that in the West underwent recent structural and psychological modifications, which often concealed them from casual eyes. Lack of the countervailing powers that would have grown naturally out of a historical foundation had one existed made it possible for members of the Russian political class of the 1990s to import from the West only those elements of modern capitalism that suited best their personal likes and interests, what suited best their own ideas of how an economy should be organized after the decades-old system of the command economy was disposed of.[1]

In other words, when Russia embraced so-called market reforms that supposedly were to take the economy to the promised land of Western-style capitalism, the "reforms" turned out to be devoid of some vital parts. These included the force of tradition and social experience that would make the economy resistant to infections of irresponsible greed. But the "reforms" did include vast powers over consumers and workers for political and business authorities, who exhibited total disregard for public interests. The result was predictable: when building its new capitalist economic system, Russia often adopted, as has been the case in politics, the most primitive, most cynical, and morally basest options.

In the example of Russia we can see how one of many material trends in the West can be transformed into the key issue of another country and become the fundamental pillar of the emerging economic system. In this chapter I will characterize the underlying features of this distinctive form of capitalism that has taken roots in my country and will probably prevail here for many years.

Economy of Power and Pure Chance

After the formal completion of the "transition period" in the 1990s, Russia remained to a great extent at the start of the path toward a Western form of capitalism. After twenty-plus years on that path, Russia still lacks the economic mechanisms of a developed market economy that had been the stated main goal of the reforms.

Russia nowadays is a country possessing a mixed economy, but in a different sense of the term than applies in contemporary economic theory. What is mixed in the Russian economy is the logic of economic and social behavior, rather than the forms of property and control. Russian reality combines something akin to capitalism with something totally different from capitalism. Let us have no illusions: Russia is not a democracy based on rule of law. At the same time, it is not a hard-core dictatorship, even though it may appear so sometimes, nor is the country in the stranglehold of a criminal mafia.[2] It could be characterized as a society that lives by rules that include a little bit of everything—power of law, force of habit, arbitrary politics, and criminal coercion. Russian society does not follow any clear and logical guidelines but instead adheres to certain implicit "understandings" that cannot be reduced to a single, coherent system and that at the same time are in a state of permanent evolution. You will find only one constant —a general rule of life in Russia that brings to heel everyone and everything today: the assumption that everything depends on chance and power.

Even in the 1990s Russian economic reality could not be characterized as a transition from a "socialist" planned economy to a market economy; today, such a description is absurd. Many relations and institutions, which are part of Russia's Soviet and even pre-Soviet legacy, are completely incompatible with present-day perceptions of effective market economies and exist in today's Russia not as relics of the past but rather as full-fledged components of Russia's current economic system.

At a macroeconomic level, the symbiosis of corrupt officials and opaque business practices remains a systemic factor that determines the use of a significant portion of national resources. Within the framework of this alliance, piles of cash are spent on undeclared payments to the bureaucracy by major business structures in exchange for administrative decisions that yield business profits several times over. The movement of financial resources between sectors, industries, and regions is determined not by the market or by an open and transparent political process; instead, everything is decided by backroom deals and plotting by the inner circle of the elite in power.

At a microeconomic level, the business environment in Russia today is not indicative of a coherent transition from the "administrative planned economy" of the totalitarian Soviet state to a modern ("normal") Western society; instead, it consists of a grotesque mix of institutions and diverse relations of different types: modern and traditional, market and nonmarket, legal and illegal, based on civic relations and on violence, and so on.

Ask any Russian businesswoman (or businessman) about the rules governing her life and work—and with all sincerity she will be unable to give a clear answer, even for herself. This is primarily because no universal rules in Russia can guarantee a businessperson's success and relative security— or that of any socially active Russian. In some cases the businesswoman acts on the basis of official law, in other instances she depends on the power of the authorities or on the inertia of established ties, and in still other instances she instinctively feels her way to the behavior required by circumstances.

If we now arrange these eclectic and frequently irrational actions into some system of social relations, we can articulate a number of doctrines that characterize Russia's social and economic system.

1. The Role Played by Informal Relations and the Gap Between Legislation and Economic Reality

The "game" in the economy is played not by law but by rules that evolved in the first ten to fifteen years after the collapse of the Soviet economy, which, because of the threat of spontaneous "sanctions," are observed more or less by all participants in economic activity. At the same time, official legislation works within the limits, and to the extent that it does not contradict the norms of economic behavior established spontaneously. This mix of rules and the economic activity performed in accordance with these rules is accurately described as an "informal economy," which accounts for at least half of the gross national product in Russia.

The more widespread "shadow economy" is narrower, that term referring primarily to transactions for which official registration, reporting, and taxation are avoided. The "informal economy" is broader, including activity that is not necessarily hidden but still takes place outside of or in violation of legally established guidelines—for example, the use of sham payment defaults, illegal or exotic forms of payment, understatement or overstatement of valuations and prices, false exports, the use of undue benefits, and so on. These relations are prevalent in the part of the economy that is concealed from accounting and taxation, but also to a large extent in public activity. The unofficial economy does not exist separately from the official or legal economy. Rather, it permeates the legal economy, introducing corrections and peculiarities in the behavior of firms that are inexplicable in terms of legislation and official rules for economic activity.

2. The Role of Unofficial Coercion

The functioning of the informal economy inevitably depends on an "informal" system of power. Russia's economy, society, and state have all started to live by unwritten rules, under which citizens (in particular socially active people) and even official agencies do not act on the basis of law but operate instead on the basis of personal relations, precedents, the ability to coerce, and the like.

The ability of an entity to lobby in favor of its economic interests in a confrontation with conflicting interests is often decisive. Technical legality may be observed or ignored. The method of coercion may consist of the power of official administration, effective control over a market or its subjects, or direct (criminal) violence, but in any case the essential "law" is the law of the strongest.

3. The Role of Mediation

Government is incapable of acting as impartial mediator in economic disputes or as guarantor of contract execution. This function must instead be assumed by the economic subjects themselves, each relying solely on its own strength relative to that of its adversaries, or on the power of its patrons.

4. The Role of Trust

As the performance of obligations is not regulated by the state but depends rather on the strength of economic agents, a systemic lack of trust prevails. Business owners and traders do not trust the state, and the state authorities do not trust business. Banks do not trust clients, or clients the banks, and enterprises do not trust their creditors and partners. The public trusts no one (although it naturally has to interact with both the state and business) and is increasingly coming to consider this is the normal and natural condition for society. As a result, Russian companies inevitably have less room to maneuver economically than typical corporations in the developed world, and each company is accorded far fewer opportunities.

5. The Role of Concentrated Economic Power

The need for businesses to use their own resources to guarantee the performance of obligations and to rely on the "informal justice" of necessity begets a highly concentrated, quasi-monopoly entrepreneurial structure. At least 70 percent of the gross product is controlled by two or three dozen business structures, with decisions adopted by several hundred people constituting the business and administrative elite in Russia. From this perspective the notorious "oligarchy," which includes businessmen who are formally unrelated to the state administration and the heads of major state and quasi-state corporations, as well as officials overseeing business on behalf of the state, is not an embarrassing error or a temporary phenomenon of the transitional period in Russia but rather the natural consequence of the economic and political system of the country.

6. The Role of Property Rights

Neither compliance with the law, nor comparatively honest business practices, nor even compliance with unwritten rules ("understandings") can guarantee that private property will not be "redistributed" or confiscated by someone with more powerful economic, political, or administrative connections. If a group of powerful people actually controls a territory, industry, or infrastructure, it can easily seize the rights of the owners of all manner of assets by using biased or subordinate arbitration courts, filing fictitious bankruptcies, or engaging in sabotage through administrative agencies or the company's employees. High-profile conflicts over specific enterprises that are intermittently publicized in the media represent no more than the tip of the iceberg in the permanent transfer of control over property for reasons unrelated to economic management of this property.

Peripheral Capitalism

Despite its eclecticism and seeming lack of viability, the system actually has an intrinsic stability and is capable of self-propagation and even distinct progress, as is illustrated by the system's relative successes in 2001–2008. Moreover, the system has secured its own political and social support—extremely reliable support—through the establishment of a large web of influential people and groups that extract considerable personal gain in return.

This social support is not limited to high-ranking state officials and businessmen close to them but embraces a wide range of different interest groups. Their interaction determines the actual situation in the economy, and they benefit from the results of this interaction, but they are only partially linked to official power structures at different levels. One key factor —actual control over resources, from economic territories and infrastructure assets to the working-age population and money—enables a specific group to participate in the organization of Russian economic life and accordingly extract personal gain.

Interest groups can be established on the basis of various principles: territorial, sector-specific, corporate, clan, and so on. They may have varying degrees of internal integration and disparate structural forms. They can represent the official executive authorities, quasi-official structures, including public monopolies at different levels (like Gazprom, Transneft, and other state-controlled companies that are entrusted with monopolistic rights or mandates to regulate market conditions on the federal level, and similar regional companies). Interest groups can also represent diverse financial structures with differing degrees of state participation or without any such participation, as well as criminal gangs.

Despite the variety of forms, all these structures possess two principal features: control over vital economic resources and the predominantly non-economic, administrative nature of this control. Control over resources is demonstrated primarily by the physical ability to facilitate or impede their use to extract revenues or other benefits. Moreover, control is based less on legal property rights than on the ability to coerce anybody refusing to recognize the rights of a group to corresponding control. The forms of coercion may be direct or indirect, legal or illegal, but in the end they can be summed up as the ability to exert economic pressure or direct violence.

These structures have another distinguishing characteristic: members of the interest groups rarely generate revenues directly from use of the economic resources. They restrict themselves primarily to granting other organizations usage rights to these resources, receiving in exchange rental income (in the form of deductions, bribes, "fees," regular and irregular extortion, and so on). Naturally, this does not mean that all senior officials take bribes and embezzle state funds—the system is built in such a way that makes it possible to leverage the advantages of administrative office in more subtle, technically legal ways. But however it is accomplished, gains are derived from affiliation to a specific corporate community and not from actual production.

In fact, virtually all the current Russian elite are in some way part of groups that derive significant nonproduction revenues from the existing system and are accordingly interested in preserving it. These are officials capable of profiting from adopting economic and political decisions that benefit different groups, captains of big business able to pay bribes and obtain in exchange monopoly income. These are officers of law-enforcement agencies that control the security forces, capable of protecting business from criminals outside the system and at the same time acting as extortionists—criminals inside the system. Finally, this includes the leaders of the mass media and professional politicians inside the system (members of parliament, leaders of public organizations supporting the system) who provide ideological protection for the system and exploit the contradictions within the elite to extract corporate and personal gain. The ubiquity of ties between different interests in the system makes it clear that the Russian elite could not destroy the system without sustaining losses, even if it perceived the vulnerability of the system and historical dead end implicit in it.

These are the general traits of contemporary Russian capitalism. Extensive academic and journalistic investigations have accorded Russian capitalism a variety of titles based on different attributes: "bureaucratic," "criminal-bureaucratic," "*nomenklatura* capitalism." I do not consider these terms appropriate. First, they are emotional and subjective. Second, they reflect and highlight only one of numerous important features of Russian capitalism and fail to express adequately its complex and contradictory nature.[3] The term *peripheral capitalism* is more appropriate for today's Russia.

On the one hand, such a definition unambiguously reflects the dearth in Russia of a mature civil society and inherent institutions, in particular, an effective judicial system, with honest and independent courts; a competitive political system rather than the existing decorative party-parliamentary apparatus; and a government that is accountable to parliament and to the parties. On the other hand, the word *peripheral* stresses the absence of self-sufficiency and integral mechanisms for growth in the Russian economy and the high degree of dependence of Russia's economy and business on the nucleus of modern capitalism (that is, the economically developed part of the world), a dependence that was, by the way, clearly demonstrated during the Great Recession.

Revolution or Restoration?

Incidentally, we should take into account such incontrovertible aspects of the political system in Russia today as 1) an authoritarian but basically weak state; 2) the special role of one or two of its top leaders, who stand far above the rest of the leadership and the clans competing for influence with the top leaders; 3) the semifeudal relations within the state apparatus (the allocation of positions, a system of "feeding troughs" that by mutual understanding will be used as a source of illegal income, and so on). We may to a certain extent even refer to restoration of the system that existed in Russia before 1917: a "peripheral" capitalism that accorded an excessive role to a bloated bureaucracy and was enveloped by an authoritarian monarchy and by the explicit fragility of the institutions of a civil society.

The Russian economy also retains many of the traits that were characteristic of backward Russian capitalism (compared with the system in western

Europe), with its dependence on the more advanced economies, at the start of the twentieth century. The backbone of the economy is based now, as it was then, on primary natural resources (extraction and processing of minerals, agriculture, fishing, and forestry) and also on a tertiary sector (transportation and communications, trade, and financial services) that operates in a limited market defined primarily by the needs of the first sector. Everything else consists either of small-scale manufacturing, sales and distribution companies with little capacity for growth or of isolated cases of well-managed high-tech companies. Optimists view these rare gems as precursors of large-scale modernization. Most of the country's producers, however, are hamstrung by inertia and an inability to optimize production and improve cost-effectiveness.

The actual use of the country's economic resources also mirrors the situation at the start of the twentieth century. Just as it was a century ago, Russia is plagued by low mobility of labor (in all senses—territorial, professional, and social), low intensity of land use, and extremely weak development of capital markets, compared with those of the West.

Despite the existence of a stock market that from the outside appears appropriately structured, no Russian companies have used it to obtain significant funding. Those that have borrowed through stock market tools have almost exclusively turned to foreign exchanges. Nor has the Russian stock market been used for hostile takeovers, as such a maneuver would be impossible even technically, because virtually all Russian companies with listed shares have a free float of less than 10 percent. Because significant dividends are paid to outside shareholders only in exceptional force-majeure circumstances, Russia's stock exchanges have never played the role of capital markets. They have instead simply been a decorative feature and fraudulent tool for the reallocation of the money of state companies and the public in favor of "stock market professionals."

Money markets in Russia also bear little resemblance to full-fledged capital markets. The credit facilities of private commercial banks have been used primarily by small and medium businesses. Large loans capable of pumping capital into other spheres and industries are provided by two or three large state credit institutions or (far more frequently) by foreign bank syndicates—which explains why the foreign corporate debt of Russian companies exceeded USD 500 billion in 2008. A complete national capital market was not created in Russia in the formative period of Russian capitalism in the late nineteenth and early twentieth centuries, and it still hasn't during its reincarnation in the late twentieth and early twenty-first centuries.

Russia has, in essence, approached the end of the first decade of this century in much the same way as it did the eve of World War I a century ago. This is a country with an economic system that is capitalist in form but that remains in the thrall of precapitalist relations. It comprises a small and weak business community, a bureaucracy that is acutely aware of its unlimited ability to control both business and society, and a supreme leader above all these groups whose power formally is indisputable and boundless but is in practice constrained by an inability to control the actions of the bureaucracy. This is a country with a nondiversified economy that is dependent on foreign markets, with an underdeveloped capital market and poor incentives for private investment. In addition, it is a country with vast natural economic resources but without strong institutions to protect the rights of the owners of these resources (the state, in many cases) or to ensure that economic agents have rapid and unimpeded access to these resources at reasonable and fair prices.

This shortcoming has a worrying implication that should haunt leaders of the Russian political class. The system that is being restored in Russia collapsed in 1917, ruining the centuries-old empire and all its institutions, leading to the temporary collapse of Russian statehood. The Soviet empire built on its ruins took tons of human flesh and blood as construction material. It collapsed in 1991 for much the same reasons, and that event shattered the basic institutions of Russian statehood for a second time in a century. If the current political and economic system in Russia proves not to be viable under new conditions and collapses under its own weight for the third time in modern history, it might bring an end to the thousand-year history of the Russian state, with tragic consequences not only for the country but for the world at large.

Crisis in Russia: Imminent and Expected

Russia, as part of the global capitalist economy, was bound to experience a strong impact from the Great Recession. The lack of effective public institutions and the vulnerability of the psychological mood of the business community, above all in terms of confidence about its own future and respect for property rights, were bound to make this impact more devastating than in more mature Western economies.

Already in late 2007 and early 2008 it was evident that a crisis in the

Russian economy was imminent. Indeed, if we proceed from the premise that a crisis is the most natural way of resolving contradictions between restraints in production and unjustifiably high production costs, preconditions for the crisis in the Russian economy had been growing visibly for several years.

For example, appreciation of the national currency, which brought the ruble's market rate quite near to the level of purchasing power parity, undermined competitiveness of domestic producers versus imports. A reduction in import duties had a similar impact: by 2008 customs duties of meaningful size had been retained for only an insignificant group of products. As there were no serious barriers to the aggressive replacement of domestic production with imports, the latter grew 30–40 percent annually. Imports have come to occupy a dominant share in nearly all market segments, from cars and food to large industrial equipment, with importers benefiting most from rising individual earnings and the increasing revenues of enterprises, absorbing most of the increase in purchasing power.

What attempts were made to curb domestic costs yielded no results. The rising prices of commodity exports generated a flow of "easy" money, with all suppliers of goods or services to exporters, including some of a corrupt and criminal nature, grabbing a slice at each stage. Acquisition of real estate as the dominant form of investing large personal savings sparked a surge of property prices, rent rates, and all types of administrative and corruption costs in the construction sector.

Excessive concentration of financial and service sectors in Russia's capital (which reflected the nature of the Russian political and economic system) led to an acute shortfall in the labor force in Moscow and an abrupt increase in salaries first in the capital and then in production zones in the provinces. The most mobile part of the labor force moved to Moscow, attracted by the promise of high incomes in the service sectors.

Energy and commodity prices rapidly grew because of rising world prices and the resulting shortfall on the domestic market. Price hikes were also provoked by the government's reluctance (or inability) to control costs at state-controlled monopolies or restructure them with a view to promoting competition. Key monopolies remained just as opaque and resistant to effective government control as they had been five or ten years earlier.

At the same time, the government's ability to influence the economic situation, despite an impressive increase in tax collection, has not grown materially. Rapid growth in the money at its disposal was accompanied by a de facto decrease in the government's quality and functionality. While the size of the bureaucratic apparatus and the proportion of the economy it controlled grew, corruption increased rapidly, judicial and representative powers increasingly resembled mere scenery, and the effectiveness of government declined in every respect, including economic policy.[4]

The efficiency of government economic policy bodies has clearly deteriorated, as has its ability to adjust and react to signals and commands coming from policy decision makers. As the overall flow of financial resources increased, the main trends and proportions of economic growth were determined more and more by the force of inertia and the vested interests of economic and bureaucratic clans, rather than by a conscious plan of economic policy makers. An economically significant reduction in the scale of corruption was dismissed as unattainable.

As a result, the impressive growth in revenues primarily facilitated an increase in imports and capital flight. Long-term investments in production facilities have been kept to the minimum. The consumer market yielded almost without a struggle to importers: the share of domestic production in consumption patterns contracted rapidly in almost every product group with the exception of alcohol, some construction materials, and basic electronics.

Dubious practices have been extended to enterprises with government participation. Leveraging unprecedented levels of borrowing, large state companies have been buying assets in the private sector and have been actively taking part in highly controversial financial investments. Control over financial flows in this sector has fitted more and more with the logic of a functioning parallel economy. Positions in this sector were filled by managers, whose numbers grew like mushrooms, from sectors unrelated to business activity.

The concerns of major owners in the private sector also grew in size and gravity, which manifested itself in persistent attempts to transfer the core of their businesses outside the country, and to avoid showing political ambitions or attracting any publicity in Russia. The media abound with evidence of this. The process has been visible to professional observers of Russian business life since 2006 at the latest.

By 2008 all the preconditions for the start of the crisis, primarily overstated prices set by key economic agents, became visible. So when the situation in a number of Western financial institutions sharply deteriorated in August of 2008, it precipitated acute capital flight from Russia, triggering turmoil in the Russian financial sector followed by the protracted economic crises of 2008–2009.

The Blessing of Underdevelopment

On the formal side, the global slump dealt Russia a painful blow. Contraction of manufacturing production was perhaps most serious, its scope and depth larger than in any other country with an economy of a comparable size. Production fell by more than 10 percent, and in some industries it plunged to 60 percent of the precrisis levels, in spite of the fact that national currency depreciated some 40 percent against the dollar and the euro. The fall in the price of oil and natural gas, on which more than half of the Russian federal budget depends, made inevitable sharp curtailment of the government investment and current spending. Investment schemes in the private sector also suffered severe cuts, primarily in the extraction and metals sectors, in view of complete uncertainty about future prices and other parameters, coupled with growing difficulties with debt financing for investment programs.

Nevertheless, the consequences of the crisis proved to be less grave than one might have feared. After an active phase from mid-September 2008 to February 2009, capital flight settled at comparatively low levels, the ruble exchange rate stabilized, and the era of imported inflation came to an end. Revenue growth stopped, but overall revenues did not decrease materially. Unemployment increased but was moderate in scale, and did not lead to an abrupt or protracted drop in consumer activity, except in depressed regions and cities that were dependent on one industry and were thus disproportionately affected by the recession. In general, consumption of a range of disposable goods and services for the country as a whole was only down a few percentage points, while only the sales of comparatively expensive durable goods, above all new cars, contracted by 30–40 percent.

The tertiary sector, whose fate had evoked serious misgivings from economists, adapted comparatively easily to the new conditions after the first wave of falling demand. It increased the proportion of sales from the lowest price segment and cut costs through rationalization of the product range and additional services. It so happened that the sector was less dependent on short-term and medium-term bank loans, which suddenly became far less accessible in autumn 2008, than most experts had assumed. There were no mass closure of stores and service enterprises and no accompanying layoffs. Comparatively small retail chains that had expanded rapidly by means of loans (primarily mobile retailers and digital electronics stores) were acquired by larger companies, with virtually no impact on sales levels. The most vulnerable micro-outlets in a recession, small outlets in large trading centers, had been consigned by bigger and more dynamic structures before 2008 to the most remote periphery of the trade and service sectors. As a result, their difficulties had virtually no adverse impact on the general picture of this segment in the Russian economy.

The situation was more dramatic in construction and real estate sales, which experienced the most material reduction in demand. Many developers could repay creditors only if they rapidly found new, more solvent, and wealthy owners. Nevertheless, buyers appeared for these potentially profitable assets, and the high-profile scandals and bankruptcies anticipated by many people never happened.

Paradoxical as it may seem, the fundamental weaknesses of Russian capitalism acted as a cushion, mitigating the adverse impact of the financial crisis on the Russian economy (although it should also be acknowledged here that the rapid intervention of the Russian monetary authorities in the situation played a fairly positive role).

In particular, as the stock market in Russia played and continues to play an essentially decorative role, the immense decline in activity on this market and falling prices of securities trading were simply ignored by most economists and the majority of the public. The immature status of the banking sector (compared with that in the West) and the relatively low dependence of Russian small and medium-sized businesses on bank lending allowed the sector to weather the crisis of confidence more easily. The extremely modest size of portfolio investments of Russian institutional investors, as well as the small number of such investors, meant that modest cumulative losses were sustained. At the same time, the undeveloped nature of the mortgage market resulted in smaller losses for both borrowers, who suffered from the dollar's appreciation, in which most mortgages were denominated in Russia, and banks, which were adversely affected by the increasing risk of default and the falling prices of the real estate that had been provided as collateral on loans.

The country's dependence on commodity exports also helped to mitigate the impact of the crisis. Of course the drop in commodity prices was extensive. However, levels of physical volume of their consumption and exports fell immaterially if at all. As a result, physical volumes of production contracted only slightly, and the slump in foreign currency revenues due to lower prices was partially offset by the appreciation of this foreign currency as a result of the controlled devaluation. All these factors, taken together, explain why we did not see numerous reports about the shutdown of production facilities and mass layoffs. Meanwhile, the contraction in domestic demand for imports that had rapidly accounted for an increasing share of the market, attributable to devaluation, played into the hands of less competitive domestic producers.

Finally, even the flaws in the Russian political system acted as a short-term buffer that partially mitigated the onslaught of the crisis. For example, the corrupt bureaucracy swallowed it as a minor unpleasantness, necessitating a temporary and immaterial drop in diverse forms of personal income, while the political inertia and distinctive fatalism of the population enabled the authorities to survive this period without mass protests and civil unrest.

Russian Specifics

In Russia the crisis buffeted an immature form of capitalism designated here as peripheral capitalism. This explains the specific nature of its impact on the economy, where falling prices on global commodity markets were the key negative factor, rather than the existence of distressed assets in the financial sector, primarily in banking. Consequently, the time frame of the slump, its phases, and the extent of its impact inevitably differed from corresponding crisis parameters in the West.

Unlike in the United States and western Europe, the poor quality of regulation of corporations in the financial sector is at best remotely connected to the crisis in Russia. The country had experienced a bubble primarily in the consumer and real estate sectors rather than in the financial services industry.

In the West the problems were related primarily to the exaggerated expectations of consumers, who wanted to consume more and more, despite their growing debt to the financial sector and the poor quality of their financial assets. By contrast, in Russia the exaggerated demands of producers probably had the most impact, as they kept raising their prices (and continue to do so) despite obvious demand constraints. In the United States and Europe the resumption and stimulation of domestic demand is viewed widely as the only way out of the Great Recession. In Russia, by contrast, only the revival of external demand and growth in foreign sales will enable the main business groups to regain financial health and return to growth policies.

At the same time, however, the development of domestic demand is extremely important for Russia. The country should be using the financial reserves accumulated over the past few years to implement large-scale residential housing and road construction projects and facilitate the transfer of title to land en masse to private developers and for the construction of the requisite infrastructure in the eastern territories. Despite the exceptional economic, social, and political significance of such enterprises, however, the authorities are afraid of launching major national projects, especially if they can be overseen by the public. The present administration prefers what it perceives to be a safer option: to wait passively for the world economy to extricate itself from the slump and to combine such a stance with a propaganda campaign against the West. This illustrates perfectly that the systemic flaws of the peripheral system—corruption, clan structures, lack of separation of power, and authoritarianism—constitute an insurmountable obstacle to the achievement of the principal national goals of modernization and progress.

Finally, and this is a key distinction: the West is confronted by the need to reduce the influence on the government of private business groups that have in the past successfully lobbied for the parochial interests of the financial sector, and to enable the government to regain the public nature of their role and correct past failures. By contrast, Russia is confronted by the need to create a public government. As I have tried to explain, there has never been a public government in Russia, neither at the start of the Putin era, nor in the Yeltsin days, not even under the Romanov dynasty. What we have today in Russia is essentially a compromise between an executive office of the head of state and a club of representatives from influential economic and political clans who perform the role of intermediaries between the peak of the power pyramid and its core backbone.

Therefore in the Russian case, however specific and distinctive it may be, the core of the economic problem ultimately lies, just as in the case of Western economies, in the conditions that extend beyond the area of economics and even politics. They are directly related to the motivations and principles of the country's political and business leaders—that is, their moral attitudes and goals—which could not be altered by a change in fiscal or monetary policy. In the final analysis, their spiritual aspirations and motivations for self-restraint matter more than economic education or the set of practical policies that may be imposed from outside or made out of expediency.

6

Lessons from the Crisis in a Globalized World

Morality as the Key to Survival

Postindustrial Postmodern

Returning now from a consideration of the Russian crisis to the global economy as a whole, it is hard to shake off the sensation that a very specific and extremely complicated situation has emerged over the past twenty years for the developed world. In Chapter 3 I argued that mainstream business in developed countries has come increasingly to resemble a black box, where goods or services are produced with the assistance of opaque technologies but are promoted as high-tech and innovative and consequently sold at prices that bear little relation to actual expenses.

The apotheosis of this trend appears in the accelerated and bloated growth of the financial sector. The sector has clearly exceeded the boundaries of its original mission of optimizing the allocation of economic resources and has become an independent business segment, capable of generating need and demand, and of meeting this demand by producing financial products able to generate new demand and new products. The chains of derivatives have been continuously extended, thereby creating colossal pyramids of diverse financial products, increasing the flow of money and simultaneously expanding the range of intellectuals involved with this segment. The boundaries on the possible reallocation of the domestic product to the benefit of this sector have been stretched even further, begetting what is now commonly called financial capitalism.

Furthermore, this process has not limited itself to the financial sector. Developed economies as a whole are embarking on a new stage associated by some sociologists (Jean Baudrillard, to give one example) with the concept of postmodernism. At this stage, the content of economic activity, if understood as satisfaction of reasonable and conscious needs of the consumer in an understandable and rational manner, is gradually assuming a subordinate role to satisfying instilled wants or social ambitions of consumers.[1]

Numerous extra links have become evident in the chains between producers and suppliers of basic economic resources (labor, capital, technologies) and between producers and consumers, links that were originally used to help producers meet the needs of consumers in the most rational and cost-effective manner. Logistics, accounting, design, advertising, marketing, public relations, and other ancillary functions have developed into separate industries, recruiting customers from established businesses. At the same time, these new industries along with their clients serve as customers for suppliers of other business services, such as research and consulting firms, legal offices, and the like.

As such new links grew in number and scope, becoming ever more complex and filled with advanced content, their original rationale increasingly came to be blurred and sometimes disappeared altogether, while the links themselves acquired some independent raison d'être. They provided a convenient and far more effective way of making money (in terms of the cost/benefit ratio) than the facilities originally determined for user requirements from which these links originally sprang. So instead of optimizing total costs, they rather turned into a powerful tool for redistributing total income of the society in favor of certain groups and individuals. That in its turn revived some of the once-forgotten theories that not all kinds of business activities could be regarded as producing real value contributing to society's prosperity and welfare.[2]

The economic liberalism of the 1980s–1990s derived from a different notion: that any activity generating revenue is real economic activity, constituting a full-fledged component of domestic product. Taken to a logical extreme, this means that any revenue received by economic agents implies that they (or property that belonged to them, including intellectual property) had provided services, the value of which is determined exclusively by the size of the revenue it generated and is totally unrelated to its content.

If we accept this thesis, then we must admit that no value-based judgment can be applied to the problem of what should be produced and traded by economic agents, that the only possible criterion for telling good from bad, efficient from inefficient, and true from false is the amount of revenue and profit received. Such an approach—call it Realeconomik if you will—leaves no place for moral judgment or value-based regulation, becoming a sort of reincarnation of Hegel's statement that "what is actual is rational." If an activity brings in revenues and profit, it should be considered both rational and necessary, provided it is waged within the boundaries of legality.

Moreover, there is an underlying temptation here to consider anything that generates significant profits to be effective, efficient, and accordingly moral as well (or at worst morally neutral). Under this logic, businesses that employ deceptive tactics to mislead consumers and exploit their incompetence or psychological weaknesses should not be admonished. They are simply replacing the principle of "every good or service rendered should be adequately compensated" with "everything that is paid for is a good, and its value is determined solely by the size of the payment."

To take the argument still further, acknowledging that the most effective modus operandi involves the generation of maximum revenues at minimum cost should bring us to the conclusion that the ideal business activity is to generate revenues from such "intellectual property" as brand names and techniques for tapping consumer awareness and artificially indoctrinating demand and standards for consumers. In these cases the costs of the "producer" of such products can be close to zero, while revenues may approach infinity, and accordingly effectiveness, understood as the cost/benefit ratio, can attain fantastic proportions.

But most people resist this line of thinking—except for those who make their living that way. A good example is provided by the recent public indignation over the astronomical salaries and bonuses paid to investment bankers, investment fund managers, auditors and rating agency analysts, and specialists responsible for the development of new, ever more complex and opaque financial products and schemes, and to the marketing, advertising, and public relations gurus promoting these products on appropriate markets—in short, to all the heroes of "financial capitalism" who are blamed today for the Great Recession. In terms of the logic of the "new economy" and its notion of efficiency, these people are rather the role models for achieving the greatest cost effectiveness, capable of generating colossal revenues, if not out of thin air, then out of a substance close to that.

From the viewpoint of purely economic (or, rather, business) thinking, there evidently is not a single consideration that could justify such negative public reaction on the rising proportions of the "new economy" or on large and extra-large incomes of those employed in it. The only satisfactory explanation for the public's response is moral revulsion. Whatever economic theory may have to say on the subject, most people instinctively believe that there is a difference between people's real wants, which are self-evident and can be reasonably explained, and false wants imposed on them by aggressive advertising and slick persuasion.

This inversion of logic is of fundamental importance and not at all an abstract matter. We fundamentally reject all contributions of morality to economic relations when we believe that any money-making methods, from the manufacture of foodstuffs to the supply of services—whether those of a stock market analyst or of the developer of a new brand of handkerchiefs—are equally valuable for the prosperity and development of society and the economy. To be more precise, we abandon the connection between morality and economic relations when the value of a product is determined exclusively by the money that its producers can extract from the economic agents around them.

It's worth taking note here of the nature of the objections against treating dubious kinds of economic activities on an equal footing with those satisfying vital needs of the society, or developing intellectual and spiritual capabilities of its members. These objections may seem to be of a purely moral nature, but in a longer perspective they also bear direct relation to economic efficiency. If we focus attention on social rather than individual well-being and development, we see that things contradicting moral sense and values that evolved through history cannot be efficient or productive. And that seems only natural: as human values historically evolved into spiritual norms and objectives contributing to the survival and growth of human communities, by definition they could not be economically counterproductive. In this sense things moral are at the same time highly pragmatic, if seen within a sufficiently long span of time. Morality, one might say, is a long-term version of pragmatic approach, and thus could well be a factor of economic productivity and efficiency, helping to select and support the kinds of economic activities that will inevitably make the economy as a whole better suited to the needs of society and hence more productive and efficient.

Over the past two or three decades, however, the aggressive advance of the opposite mindset, the Realeconomik approach, has been more visible, and that has led to many negative consequences for the sustainability of national economies, their ability to withhold all manner of shocks, and their overall efficiency.[3]

Return to Meaning

The economy (and this also holds true for politics) inevitably pays a price, and in many cases a high price if moral criteria are abandoned or disparaged. As the lessons of the economy as a whole reveal, the cost effectiveness of business activity is directly dependent on the stability and efficacy of moral principles in society and business. This dependence is established by the mechanism of confidence and trust between economic agents, without which successful market capitalism is impossible. However, it is by no means limited to this mechanism and has a far broader and diverse character.

Therefore the blurring of moral constraints constitutes a threat to objective public interest and goals, and also puts at risk sustainable economic growth, as demonstrated by the crisis. People need to understand that the Great Recession of the start of the twenty-first century is only one episode in a long narrative. The recession set the ball rolling and provided us with an opportunity to consider how to create the requisite conditions for sustainable and healthy economic growth. Nevertheless, for the time being there are no grounds for stating that the world has changed or will be different once it recovers from economic meltdown.

Structural shifts in contemporary capitalism described in previous chapters are not the product of the evil intentions of individuals—Bernie Madoff, for example, or Joseph J. Cassano, the former head of the Financial Products unit at AIG—but rather of the evolution over many years of a world system. The problem is not Madoff or Cassano or their class—such schemers have always been with us and would be even if the global financial scene were to be restructured. The problem is how to bring the hundreds of Madoffs and Cassanos under the aegis of a system of legal and moral constraint, how to direct the intelligence and energy of young, ambitious, and talented people hungry for success into channels more compatible with the ideals of public good, sustainable prosperity, and fair conditions for all people. That is the real problem—not Madoff, AIG, Lehman Brothers, or their ilk.

For the time being, however, there is no global consensus on actual prescriptions for modifying the direction of the transformations I have discussed. Strictly speaking, at this stage it remains unclear whether there is sufficient influence to drive through such change and whether these forces have sufficient political will to start steering the enormous world economic vessel in a different direction.

But the debate itself is extremely important: in the wake of the crisis, with the need to reform both the international financial system and capitalism as a whole manifest, will we return (and again I use the terms of Chancellor Merkel and President Sarkozy) from financial capitalism to productive capitalism, or continue to follow the general mood among Western elites in the opposite direction?

I hope that the widespread condemnation of "financial capitalism" in early 2009 reflects a profound shift in the consciousness of the global elite. This shift would involve a recognition that the economy will suffer serious problems in the long run if we continue to denigrate moral principles when regulating the economy and if we disregard such criteria as common sense and public benefit when assessing economic activity and its effectiveness. The opposite also holds true: if the goal is to make the world economic system strong and resistant to volatility and other destabilizing factors, then economic activity must comply not only with formal quantitative demands but also with qualitative requirements arising from moral norms.

The need to reform the international financial system debated at the peak of the crisis, as serious as it is, is just one element—an essentially technical one—of the shift required. The decision-making process will probably be modified at the IMF and perhaps at the World Bank; to a certain extent the capabilities and responsibilities of international financial institutions will be expanded. The role of the American dollar as the main international reserve currency may also be reduced to give more weight to international financial instruments, such as SDRs.[4] But these, too, are all particulars.

The main lesson of the Great Recession—the need to strengthen the role of national financial regulators—is a more fundamental task, necessitating far greater effort, but at the same time offering a greater impact in terms of stabilizing the functioning of this sector. However, even this task appears to me to be too specific if restricted to a simple tightening of existing quantitative risk criteria and more scrupulous supervision of implementation. New instructions on controlling banking transactions and on the quality of financial products are irrelevant if the general level of morality remains the same or continues to fall. Why is it assumed that the officials responsible for regulation will perform their duties conscientiously? As the Russian author Alexander Griboyedov wrote, "And who will be their judge?"[5] This question remains relevant today with respect to both governments and bureaucracies.

Morality should not be introduced into the economy through administrative fiat, but people should understand that morality is integral to all economic activity. It is impossible to promulgate special rules to support morality in economics and politics. However, if an awareness of the need for morality is encouraged, transgressions will become less acceptable and trends gradually will change. When adopting decisions, whether major or minor, whether involving legislation or not, the people involved should consider at all times the need for morality in economics and politics, and accept it as fundamental to effectiveness.

In other words, our ability to avoid such crises in the future will depend not only on increased oversight over compliance with certain quantitative norms that reflect corresponding risks. Human imagination, whipped up by the prospects of easy money, will always find a way to circumvent formal constraints. A relapse can be averted only if more stringent demands are imposed on the actual substance of activity so that we proceed on a moral basis and thereby prevent the emergence of dubious activities in the financial realm.

Naturally, this approach will encounter powerful opposition, on ideological and other grounds, but primarily because of the interest of an enormous number of people operating in these spheres to minimize or eliminate any form of regulation. Here the authorities will have to make a responsible choice: either regulate economic activity that could destabilize the economic system, or accept the fact that the system, operating contrary to public interest, will once again generate shocks similar to the financial crisis.

The Common Good and Common Threat

This choice could in principle be left to the discretion of each separate country—every society with its own history, and by virtue of such experience, its own set of values—if the world were not rapidly and irreversibly becoming interconnected through globalization: in exploitation of resources, in economic activity, and not least in politics, as manifested in the growing role of international relations.

What does this mean in practice? First, the consequences and cost of every decision adopted by the governments of developed countries grow exponentially. The consequences of abortive decisions, the cost of errors, and the responsibility of governments and leaders in deciding on specific options grow accordingly. The interdependence of economics and politics means that the actions of governments may exert a far greater influence on international development than was the case one hundred, fifty, even twenty years ago.

As a result, the responsibility for the adoption of reasonable measures has increased exponentially for all participants in international politics. The intellectual and moral demands on key political figures are becoming exceptionally high. Regrettably, today's political generation has proved incapable of meeting those demands.

Let us return to changes in international politics over the past two decades. Foreign policy has always put a premium on pragmatism, and national interests have always taken precedence over ideals and principles, all the more so as no single opinion has ever prevailed regarding the substance and boundaries of ideals and principles. Still, in the historically short period of the 1950s–1980s, many people believed that a consensus finally had been reached to move forward, gradually, step by step, sometimes retreating, but then advancing again toward international order based on specific principles rather than naked calculation for short-term gain.

International law became increasingly prominent; almost every participant in the system of international relations expressed a readiness to comply with law, if only formally or as some kind of indispensable ritual. A consensus was reached that the developed world should make an honorable effort to overcome the shameful social and economic gap dividing the world. Although change was difficult and slow to come, eventually human rights came to be understood as the highest value.[6] Leaders recognized that this value could be brought to bear on many conflicts.

But the past two decades have shown these achievements—and the principles on which they were built—to be on shaky ground, as the tenets of Realeconomik gained currency. The United States were affected most by this development. A shameless distortion of victory in the Cold War into the Fukuyama-esque "end of history" led the American elite to insist that the interests of international development and progress should conform to the interests of the United States. The lack of a second "superpower" meant that some American leaders considered as superfluous the painstaking work with its allies and with neutral states that might have nudged the country toward more principled policies.

U.S. behavior during the Cold War had been perceived differently in Russia than in America: most representatives of the official Soviet elite were convinced that the United States' declared defense of worldwide freedom, democracy, and human rights was hypocritical. The logic of opposition and the international game forced U.S. leaders to shut their eyes to many actions that were incompatible with the principles of protecting human rights. Defenders of U.S. policy would argue that the philosophical commitment it embodied is more important than isolated instances of deviation from its principles. But hypocrisy is insidious: if you wear a mask for a long time, you will find in the end that it sticks to your face. Protracted adherence to certain principles, even if it is insincere or made under duress, will at some stage make those principles a norm, accepted unquestioningly by new generations. Still, irrespective of the skepticism aroused over this issue, the ongoing conversation in international politics from the 1950s to the 1980s about principles—and the public promises to adhere to such principles—undoubtedly contributed in the long term to making the world more predictable, safer, and even more moral.

The United States' retreat from the idea of universal principles and the transition to a missionary or even messianic understanding of the nation's role in international politics—as the emphasis in the formula "We are bringing the world freedom" shifted from the final word to the first word— marked a major setback for international politics. Over the past two decades, the United States adopted an increasingly cavalier attitude toward the norms, constraints, and obligations imposed by international law. The principle of the inviolability of established borders, which had played a considerable role in curbing international conflicts and ethnic clashes after World War II, was eroded by flexible and selective application. We have also come to see serious disregard of such fundamental principles as the collective nature of international peace-keeping operations, the need for U.N. sanctions before implementing any type of "humanitarian interventions," and the importance of refusing international recognition of any unilateral acts of ethnic cleansing or separatism.

The United States' perception of having achieved an unconditional victory in the Cold War marked the starting point for the nation's gradual refutation of the principles for world order elaborated after the end of World War II. With the threat of armed conflict between two nuclear superpowers gone, the United States abandoned subtlety and recognition of the complexity of global relations. Once there was no enemy with which war had to be avoided at all costs, including self-restraint, the reasons for that self-restraint seemed gone as well. Calls to reject the Yalta model of international relations were based on a desire not to stop thinking in terms of blocs and spheres of influence but to cast off the limitations on the expansion of U.S. influence.

The stated focus of American foreign policy was the defense of the principles of freedom, democracy, and human rights. In practice, however, "the promotion of democracy throughout the world" was so selective and so tightly bound to the mercantile interests of the United States that virtually everyone outside the nation's borders interpreted the phrase to mean that opportunity and right go hand in hand—which is, incidentally, at the root of Realeconomik.

Ideology still played a specific role in the determination of foreign policy in the United States. However, as this ideology boiled down to American ideas on the appropriate world order, the positive role of ideology was minimal, while the disturbance it created in actual geopolitical calculations was real and material.

Consequently, the end of the Cold War meant that we all faced an unpleasant paradox. The "winners" exploited in full the political "spoils of war" as they developed the idea of a single world center of military and political influence. Meanwhile, the "losers" were told that, as they no longer constituted a threat, the "winners" wanted no role in their transformation or in funding such a transformation. It made more sense to forget about the former USSR, which was no longer portrayed as powerful and threatening, but was instead defined by primitive myths and rumors; news from the country was treated as postcards from the lives of savages. Gorbachev was asked to comply with material requests to forgo the use of force and democratize the USSR—and he duly complied, on the basis of his own ideas about the development of the world order. No one made any such demands of Yeltsin, even during the war in Chechnya; instead they played the following game with him: "You are deceiving us about developments at home, but we won't get involved. In exchange, we will simply ignore you wherever possible on all other issues internationally." Yeltsin (and then Putin and now Medvedev) was accorded respect as the leader of a superpower. However, he was made to understand that no one would accept Russia or its neighbors as close allies of the West: financial support was out of the question, and the old political stereotypes would survive. In contexts where it was convenient, America declared the Cold War to be over. In other contexts the war went on, in a primitive form, as if by inertia. Nothing constructive could come from this inconsistency. And now, more than twenty years after Mikhail Gorbachev and George H. W. Bush declarared the Cold War to be over, relations between the countries have reached a dead end, with no clarity and a constant sense of danger.

An integral component of values in U.S. foreign policy has been compromised. Moreover, the events of 11 September 2001 ultimately had a similar impact. The emergence of an undefined transnational terrorist group as the opponent to the United States has complicated the concept of sovereignty and the issue of constraints on international actions. The "war on terror" is a war in an undefined legal field, where the rules and the extent of any constraints have been set by the United States, based on the country's own interpretations of the expediency and admissibility of certain actions. Correct procedures were not even followed within NATO, which invoked Article 5 of the Washington Treaty on collective self-defense. The United States decided to move independently, involving allies as it deemed appropriate. The large-scale war against Saddam Hussein's Iraq—unjustified by any documented need and unsanctioned by international legitimacy— originated in this go-it-alone stance. The same approach inspired the extralegal incarceration of people suspected of terrorism, the forcible determination of the fate of the former republics and autonomous regions of Yugoslavia, and the push to expand the territory controlled by NATO to countries of the former USSR.

Even in a matter ostensibly outside the United States' remit, expansion of the European Union, some detected American fingerprints. There was probably no alternative to the political decision to rapidly include numerous countries in central and southern Europe in the European Union. However, this project was implemented superficially, with no attention to critical political and philosophical concepts. The expansion of the European Union focused on technical issues and avoided at all cost consideration of the question: "What does a political and economic Europe imply and where are its borders?" The simplified, formal nature of the expansion was underlined by the simultaneous incorporation of the same countries into NATO, a concurrence that led outside observers to link the political remit of the two ventures and to attribute a clandestine and decisive role to the United States. Subsequently the leaders of France and Germany had to resort to artistic demarches to try to prove the opposite.

The abrupt expansion of the European Union yielded invaluable benefits to new member countries. However, implementation of a "simplified structure" implied not only a bold step by the West toward its most civilized neighbors, which had been impatiently anticipating such a move, but also a retreat from long-standing fundamental principles. Meanwhile, the technical nature of the measures raised doubts about the strategic future of the great experiment of a united Europe. How could leaders have the presumption to allow the instantaneous expansion of the European Union to coincide with attempts to introduce radical administrative reforms? For it was obvious that, in contrast to the politicians, rank-and-file citizens would balk at the expansion and that it would lead to a natural burst of isolationism and "euro skepticism."

The painstaking, gradual, and largely successful transfer, coordinated with all members of the European Union, of some functions of national countries to a supranational level—work that had been performed with legal clarity and in accordance with agreed "European values"—had been violated. Expansion had one side effect: the economic and political union created as a mechanism for raising the efficiency of economic activity and administrative management in western Europe was transformed into a tool to divide the world along new borders, to create blocs based on so-called differences in civilization. In fact, this transformation of the EU had an ambiguous impact on Europe's shared values, both reinforcing and eroding them.

The historically entrenched mechanism in the European Community of a painstaking and professional search for consensus was undermined by countries that sought to aggressively defend their special interests. The quality of professional decision making fell. Meanwhile, pompous institutional projects that clearly bore the mark of bureaucratic interventions rather than substantive measures contributed to an erosion in the quality of decisions in the European Union.

Whether intentionally or not, a clear signal was also sent to the Russian elite, who had been assigned the role of the nearest enemy to "civilization," a threat meant to unify the old and new Europe. However skeptically we may assess the ability of the Russian elite to find a common language with European politicians, the ostentatious and ill-articulated erection of a military-political and economic wall between Russia and the rest of Europe on the basis of no distinct political logic promoted neither positive developments in Russia nor stability in international relations. On the contrary, the buildup of mutual grievances and suspicions makes developments in politics or economics unlikely. Unfortunately, the Christian principle that you live in one world and cannot build "heavenly riches" here for yourself alone, cutting yourself off from the rest of the world, has yielded to the eternal art of separate unions, intrigues, and connections.

Time to Think

However, the saddest aspect lies elsewhere. All the ills I have cited are also reflected domestically in every society in the world. If politics, including international relations, demonstrates a systematic retreat from moral principles and values, at a time of globalization in the postindustrial society of the twenty-first century, the world economy will always move asymptomatically toward crises. Periodically, crises will occur and may well prove even more destructive.

I have already described the perverse trends that rule in Russian society —the weakness of the institutions of civil society and state law and order, the amorphous rules of behavior in economic life, the abrupt disintegration of the role of public morality, combined with a naïve belief in the uniqueness of that society and a resentment of the rest of the world for refusing to acknowledge and respect this uniqueness—all helping to undermine the social order.

However, even in societies traditionally considered to represent the benchmark of democracy, we can perceive trends that pose a visible threat to social and moral progress. I am not even referring here to issues that tend to be raised by sensationalist journalists: the growing readiness to forsake certain civil rights and freedoms in the name of a successful battle with terrorism and other "enemies of the state," or increasing xenophobia attributed to the increasingly perceptible presence of immigrants at a time of protracted economic hardship. I am far more concerned about the creeping expansion of political and economic postmodernism that I have described: the retreat of public consciousness from the search for meaning in politics and economics, its immersion in the consumption of newer and newer artificial forms offered in abundance by the virtual "new economy" and virtual politics. This is a separate issue, but it is still true that today's Europe and the United States have evolved historically owing to a fierce struggle by their populations for its interests and ideals against external pressures. This struggle, which was supported by reason and consideration of reality on the one hand and long-established understanding of the concepts of honor, dignity, and morality on the other, created European civilization in its most positive manifestation. When those concepts are erased from public consciousness; when the public is immersed in a virtual world of indoctrinated requirements, brands, and symbols; when we become reluctant to ask where money comes from and how some people acquired so much, that civilization is in jeopardy. Political and business people are not from some higher caste. They are the same "men on the street," with the same ideas, psychology, and prejudices as the public. The degradation of mass consciousness will, after a certain time, inevitably result in the degradation of politics and business, in decay and an inability to progress.

However, this is a different story, as is the search for alternatives and unswerving belief and hope.

Conclusion

The idea of writing this book came to me as the world financial crisis began unfolding, and the writing itself was done mostly against the background of this crisis as it grew into the Great Recession of the early twenty-first century. But the crisis served only as a convenient context for making some generalizations concerning certain trends in market capitalism of recent decades. That ultimately led to an attempt to establish the role today of morality—or, alternatively, its neglect—primarily in connection with the events of the past two decades.

Since I began writing, changes may have occurred in the world markets or in the mood of investors, but the main ideas of the book cannot become irrelevant or outdated. If these ideas are false, if the situation is developing along lines completely different from what I expected, then I have wasted my time. But if they are true, they will be true a year from now or several years from now.

My impression is that events since the dramatic volte-face on financial markets in the autumn of 2008 have borne out the ideas expressed in this book. Indeed, fiscal and monetary policy measures taken since then have to a considerable extent neutralized the negative impact of a sudden surge of instability on financial markets and thus prevented a deeper and more prolonged recession in the world economy, at least for the time being. Additional liquidity and trillions of dollars of bailout and stimulus programs poured into major Western economies have made it possible to support and invigorate demand, thus mitigating the worst scenario for the world economy.

A deep reform of the system of financial regulation, however, the need for which was widely discussed and widely endorsed in the midst of the crisis, never happened. There have been sporadic attempts to improve regulation, certain bills aimed at reforming the financial sector have been approved by the U.S. Congress, but so far the system is little changed from what we saw before the crisis. Nothing that really matters has been done.

Nor has the general situation in the financial sector changed much. We have the same rating system that has been generally condemned as useless and misleading. We have the same institutional investors recklessly following the advice of "financial experts" who already helped them to lose much of their money. We hear the same voices saying that now is the right time to take chances and earn a fortune from speculations in the securities markets. It's the same people, same methods, same tactics; the only difference is a general belief (not necessarily well founded) that the worst is over and we are entering a new period of relative stability and prosperity.

Here is what Jacques Attali, a French economist and the former chief of the European Bank for Reconstruction and Development, said as recently as May 2010:

> For the past two years, in any case, we have done nothing. . . . We are paying lip service to G-20, which achieves nothing, we announce things which are never put in place, we are so scared to make the smallest decision that nothing gets done and meanwhile, the spiral continues. . . . Banks are continuing to speculate exactly as they did before, immoral actions are still going on, *nothing*, absolutely *nothing* has changed in a system which is entirely in the hands of international finance.[1]

If Attali exaggerates, the exaggeration is slight. If he is right, we cannot expect to see fundamental changes in the years to come. Calls have gone unheard for a far-reaching change in moral attitudes, for deep and meaningful reform of modern capitalism ("financial capitalism"), founded on such values as honesty, openness, social responsibility, self-restraint, and fair competition. We are not going to see fundamental changes based on wider public control, restrictive regulation of financial speculation, and a ban on aggressive marketing of questionable products. On the contrary, political and business leaders are acting on the premise that the situation will inevitably return to "normal" as it was understood before the crisis. Fundamental change is not on the agenda.

In view of that, I will risk making some projections for the future. I believe the situation in the world economy will never again be as it was in the first half of 2008. There will be no return to the high level of consumer demand fueled by middle-class consumer enthusiasm, which had been feeding the boom in the financial markets. We will still see a lot of speculation and rent-seeking activities, but they will not be able to support the kind of dynamism and ever-growing size and intensity of financial flows that we witnessed before the Great Recession.

However, the authorities and intellectual elite in the West, unable to size up the new reality and develop new mechanisms for promoting growth, will continue to cling to old tools of economic policy, and they will be misguided by the amoral tenets of what I call Realeconomik. It would be unrealistic to expect profound changes in education, management, and economic thinking, even though many may suspect that old ways are not working anymore. Keeping things as they are may make the problems look less acute for some time, but inertia will ultimately lead to serious political crisis a dozen or so years from now. Prolonged economic stagnation will inevitably bring about the crisis of political institutions and of the political balance of power.

International relations do not demonstrate any noticeable positive change, either. The trend seems to ignore ethical principles in diplomacy, to neglect positive dialogue with world public opinion, based on offering convincing moral arguments linking foreign policy measures to lofty goals and moral imperatives. Major international conflicts, which attract the lion's share of attention of the world media, increasingly look like conflicts of interest rather than conflicts of principle, and there is no reason to believe that this trend will soon be reversed. New ambitions to find solutions to old conflicts fail to produce tangible results, and hopes connected with the new U.S. administration and its promises to restructure foreign policy are gradually being replaced by increasing skepticism. International solidarity based on shared values is too weak to produce powerful concerted actions, as could be seen from the experience of the fiscal crisis in the euro zone.

The world at large, and the West as a part of it, will have to pay a high price for the inaction of its political leaders. Moreover, each further year of passivity will raise the price still higher—as happened in the financial crisis.[2] After all, the financial crisis is only a small episode in the context of the fate of world capitalism. Far more profound issues than stability in the financial sector seem to be at stake.

Modern capitalism as embodied by the West of the twentieth century has evolved more from a certain set of values and rules of behavior, which we might call capitalist ethics, than from new technologies and industrial innovations. In fact, the latter seem to be products of capitalism rather than its driving force. I have argued that ultimately it is trust, rather than production technologies, that forms the foundation of the capitalist market system and constitutes the most important condition for its efficient functioning. The logic of "postmodern" development, as I can see it, promotes all sorts of "innovations" which may improve efficiency interpreted as a simple cost/profit ratio, but which work to the detriment of trust, making the system less transparent, less comprehensible, and ultimately irresponsible. Whatever may be the benefits of the "new economy," they could not outweigh the damage, if the damage is inflicted on the cornerstone of the system—that is, on trust. And trust depends in turn on the existence of public morality. Ultimately, it is morality that makes possible all kinds of basic economic actions, including production, exchange, saving, and investment.

Taking ethical constraints out of the system inevitably leads to its degradation, and ultimately its total collapse. When technical innovations are accompanied by proliferation of immoral actions, then they in essence are ruining the system, not strengthening it. When large companies capable of influencing people's minds use their power to change human wants and attitudes to cultivate an ideal consumer for their products, they divest capitalism of its core feature, destroy the source of its vitality and social efficiency. By modifying both the form and essence of such notions central to market economy as productivity, efficiency, and fair competition, they create conditions conducive to the degeneration of capitalism.

Moreover, degeneration is not limited to the economic system. Political systems based on pluralism and competition, which have been considered among the greatest achievements of the twentieth century, are suffering devastating blows. Justification of intellectual manipulations aimed at controlling consumer behavior inevitably leads to political and social wants and preferences that also become subject to aggressive manipulation. That in its turn means the end of democracy as understood by the twentieth-century liberal intellectual tradition. In fact, we are witnessing a highly distressing development: Western democracies are fiercely fighting what they consider to be the worst cases of authoritarian rule in the Third World, and at the same time they themselves are creating at home a system of covert, or "soft," authoritarianism, under which violent suppression of political freedoms is replaced by strict control over social behavior.

On the other hand, citizens, whose insistence on higher standards is in the end the only guarantee for maintaining the general direction and standards of politics, are becoming increasingly indifferent. Apart from passionate activists who organize mass civil acts of protest, public political activity has suffered a marked decrease.

The crisis in world politics in the late twentieth century and the start of the twenty-first is primarily attributable to a broad-based departure from the fundamental humanist values contained in the Universal Declaration of Human Rights. Cynicism and hypocrisy in politics and the de facto rejection of the principles and values of the humanist tradition in political practice has weakened the system of support for the foundations of the world order and rendered the world incapable of preventing crises and ineffective in conflict resolution.

If Western societies and their political leaders are to prevent further degradation of the capitalist system and change the situation for the better, they have to shoulder responsibility and exhibit political will, and they must understand that policy based on ethical principles is the most pragmatic option in the long term. This task is truly demanding. The next five years will require a more rigorous reexamination of economics and capitalism than we have seen in the past thirty years. But ethical policy combined with independent professional expertise could counteract cynicism and restore the values of Western civilization as the driving force of economic and social development. It is the best, the safest, investment we can make in our future.

NOTES

Introduction

1. To give just one example, the former Federal Reserve Chairman Paul Volcker, addressing the annual conference of the Columbia Center for Capitalism and Society in February 2009, in the capacity of chairman of President Obama's Economic Recovery Advisory Board, spoke of "massive economic and financial crisis" that should be seen as a "challenge to capitalism and society."
2. For example, one of the conclusions of the Financial Crisis Inquiry Commission (FCIC) made public in January 2011 clearly states that "While the business cycle cannot be repealed, a crisis of this magnitude need not have occurred."

CHAPTER 1: Developments in the Global Economy

1. A fairly good description appears in Charles R. Morris, *The Two Trillion Dollar Meltdown: Easy Money, High Rollers, and the Great Credit Crash* (New York: Public Affairs, 2009).
2. A credit default swap is a contract under which the seller of credit protection agrees to pay the buyer a certain amount (as a rule, the par value net of the recovered amount of the loan) in the event of a certain credit event. In exchange, the buyer hands over the underlying obligation to the seller or pays the corresponding recovered amount. A variant of the swap involves a zero recovered price; in this case, the seller of the credit protection pays the full par value of the debt if the borrower defaults.
3. As noted in an editorial in the *Financial Times*, "people were not unaware of the risks, but both regulation and private risk management were based on the faulty premise that if each entity looks after its own risk, no one needs to about systemic risk" (9 March 2009).
4. The same *Financial Times* editorial put it this way: "Economic policymakers could have limited these dangers, but they did not do so. Instead, they allowed the bubble to inflate and let financial transactions become increasingly opaque and ever more leveraged" (Ibid.).
5. Naturally, the models, including some that were accorded countless prizes,

were accurate only within limited (critical) conditions: compliance with the law, a minimum of ethical principles and morality, and so on. If those conditions are violated, these models are useless. In other words, they are purely hypothetical concepts.

6. It was held that any analytical report, forecast, assessment of risks or investments—in short, any economics work—was justifiable only if backed by a range of special mathematical calculations and models. Otherwise, the material looked unconvincing and would fail to have the desired effect on investors: to persuade them to cough up. In fact, all this learned mathematical baggage conveniently illustrated only what economists already understood without this material. And no models would enable them to see something that they did not understand. Mathematics often merely served as advertising window dressing, creating the illusion of science and reliability. This reminds me of Lewis Carroll's Alice wondering, "And what is the use of a book without pictures or conversations?" See also "After the Crash: How Software Models Doomed the Markets," *Scientific American*, 21 November 2008, http://www.scientificamerican.com/article.cfm?id=after -the-crash.

7. The history of this kind of worldview goes back as far as Jean-Jacques Rousseau and the Utopians. But mainstream social and economic theories of the twentieth century also rest (sometimes implicitly) on the assumption that there exist certain laws of development that could be mastered by educated scholars and put to use to facilitate and control economic and social progress. Creation of an extensive system of newly designed development institutions, both national and international, could not be justified without underlying belief in the magic of human knowledge.

A good example of the somewhat naïve belief in the magic of human intellect is the illusion widely and enthusiastically shared by some American and Soviet politicians that experience gained from successful space exploration could be extrapolated to solve earthly problems. In 1980–1990 the United States and other Western countries used technological advances to secure ideological victory over communism but clearly overestimated the role of technological progress, seeing it as an omnipotent and universal tool to solve the world's political and social problems. Then, in the early years of the twenty-first century, the very possibility of bloody civil conflicts and mass brutalities was easily dismissed as "unthinkable in the age of Internet," just as in the 1910s some people honestly believed that cinema would make the world essentially better and more sympathetic.

8. I am referring here to the scandals over the bonuses received or demanded by top management at Merrill Lynch, Morgan Stanley, the Royal Bank of Scotland, and many other financial institutions.

9. A significant number of first-rate works exist on business ethics and morality. My subject, however, is less interpersonal relations or relations between

business groups at a corporate or industry level than the link between moral principles and the global financial system, the global economy, and politics.

CHAPTER 2: Capitalism, the Market, and Morality

1. After all, in nearly every culture behaviors are made illegal because they are considered immoral and antisocial, not the other way around.
2. It is not that simple, of course. In Calvinism, English Puritanism, and other hues of Protestantism, business success and accompanying wealth are not simply the logical result of hard work and diligence but are in fact interpreted as signs of God's preference. This logic suggests the very flaw that led to today's crisis in morality: the system of strict puritanical constraints disintegrated over the centuries, but the subconscious link between wealth and godliness remains firmly entrenched in the culture of the West. Hence the relative ease of the transition to a system in which profit is the universal measure.
3. Ironically, successful emigrants from China and Vietnam in the United States and their descendants, mostly Confucian or Buddhist or atheist, have demonstrated the best examples of the so-called Protestant ethic.
4. By the way, this is the argument used by advocates of the theory of evolution to explain the existence of traits in human nature that contradict the interests of an individual's survival. As humans became distinguished from the animal world as both biological and social beings, the process of natural selection reinforced traits that contributed to the survival of the community and not just the individual—family, tribe, and so on. In other words, the predisposition of community members to care not only about themselves but also about their families promoted collective survival and was selected for at a genetic level, thereby becoming part of the nature of the species.
5. It is interesting to note here that the end of the Cold War and the consequent loss of the sense of competition on the part of the Western world has led to apparent lessening of self-discipline and moral restraint in politics, which I will discuss in chapter 4. This decline gives extra weight to the argument that competition between human communities is one of the driving forces that maintain and sustain public morality.
6. "Twenty-five People at the Heart of the Meltdown," *Guardian*, 26 January 2010.
7. Alan Greenspan said in his interview to *Frankfurter Allgemeine Zeitung* in September 2007, "People believed the rating agencies knew what they were doing. And they don't." "Greenspan Slams Ratings Agencies," *Wall Street Journal* online, http://blogs.wsj.com/economics/2007/09/23/greenspan-slams-ratings-agencies/.
8. This is how an editorial in the *Financial Times* put it: "Economic policymakers could have limited these dangers, but they did not do so. Instead,

they allowed the bubble to inflate and let financial transactions become increasingly opaque and ever more leveraged" (9 September 2009).

9. Thanks to Greenspan's patronage, the derivative business increased fivefold over five years, 2002–2007.

10. A good example is a letter entitled "The Crisis," which was made public by Greenspan lately. Though advertised as containing a good deal of self-criticism and revision of previous views, the letter in effect states that there was very little that could have been done to avert the crisis before the first clear signs of it became apparent.

11. As it was said in the interview of one of the senior executives of a well-known investment bank in London, discussing the consequences of the 1998 economic crisis in Russia, "When you can count on 300 percent return, your mind turns blind to reason."

12. Many of Madoff's clients were extremely well-educated and serious people, and most of them should have sensed that there was something abnormal about the stable high level of interest payments investments with him promised. Moreover, it was revealed that close to $12 billion was withdrawn from the Madoff company accounts in 2008 by various investors, and that half that amount was removed only three months before the financier was arrested in December 2008. In other words, many investors in this structure assumed that special conditions were attributable to Madoff's position and his contacts, which enabled him to leverage insider information. It is likely that they did not personally break the law, but instead invested with Madoff because he could circumvent the law in such a way as to end up in a better position than other financiers and thereby multiply their earnings. If so many people had not been convinced that it was normal to be "more equal" before the law than others, this fraudulent scheme would not have been so broad and extensive.

13. For example, Nick Leeson spent three and a half years in a Singapore prison, where he wrote his autobiography, *Rogue Trader,* which became a best-seller. Then, as a result of his improved social status, he began giving lectures at various conferences for high fees—a fate which is far more interesting than that of a modest bank official.

CHAPTER 3 : Shifts in the Global Economy of the 1980s–2010 and Changes in the Moral and Psychological Climate

1. *Perspektivy Rossii. Ekonomicheskii i politicheskii vzgliad* [Russia's prospects: An economic and political view] (Moscow: Galleia-print, 2006).

2. I was overcome with bitterness when I participated directly in work on political and economic reforms in Russia. The mainstream was confidently driving Russia toward a quasi-market, semicriminal economic system, with all the inevitable political consequences. However, as this direction was supported by big money—IMF loans and the Washington administration—

all arguments about the theoretical errors of the economic structures that were being built, the practical dishonesty of the people implementing the policy, the corruption and even blatant abuse were ignored. No one in Moscow or in the West wanted to discuss it.

3. "In the last analysis, the question of what are true and false needs must be answered by the individuals themselves, but only in the last analysis; that is, if and when they are free to give their own answer. As long as they are kept incapable of being autonomous, as long as they are indoctrinated and manipulated (down to their very instincts), their answer to this question cannot be taken as their own." Herbert Marcuse, *One-Dimensional Man: Studies in the Ideology of Advanced Industrial Society* (Boston: Beacon, 1964), http://www.marcuse.org/herbert/pubs/64onedim/odm1.html/.

4. This assertion is hard to substantiate with figures, but much indirect evidence backs it up. For example, except for completely new industries with no history to trace (like commercial services on the Internet), there have been virtually no new additions to the list of the world's most valuable trademarks over the past two or three decades. Newcomers to traditional markets, such as those for cars or home appliances or branded foodstuffs, invariably had to acquire established brands, or their holders had to substantially expand their presence in these markets. In the car industry, for example, the Indian automaker Tata Motors has acquired the British carmaker that held the right to the name Rover, and the Chinese company Geely Automobile Holdings has bought the Swedish Volvo car corporation. In both cases the prime motive for the acquisition was the exploitation of trademarks and other intangible assets belonging to the acquired European companies. In a sense such acquisition could be viewed as an attempt to buy a historical name, which nowadays carries with it enormous revenues that are not directly related to production activities but rather represent a form of unearned income (rent) derived from the title to the historical name and the vague aura associated with it in the minds of consumers.

5. It must be admitted, however, that fraud can do far more damage in this sector than in most. Though the ten-figure dollar amounts that figured in the cases of traders Nick Leeson, Yasuo Hamanaka, and Jerome Kerviel, or the $50 billion financial pyramid of Bernard Madoff, are rare exceptions, the average size of possible embezzlements and frauds is of an order of magnitude higher here than in industries outside the financial sector.

6. Arbitrage is the simultaneous buying and selling of securities, commodities, and the like in different markets or in derivative forms in order to take advantage of varying prices.

7. Speech by Lorenzo Bini Smaghi, member of the Executive Board of the ECB, Nomura Seminar, Kyoto, 15 April 2010.

8. I fully understand that this idea involves value-based reasoning which could meet objections based on a different set of arguments. Still, I'd like to see it

discussed as it relates to the future course of economic development in the West, which I consider a topic of utmost importance.

9. International Institute for Labour Studies, *World of Work Report 2009: The Global Jobs Crisis and Beyond,* Snapshot of the United States.

10. Leigh Phillips, "Merkel and Sarkozy Call for Global 'Economic Security' Council," EUobserver.com, 9 January 2009, http://euobserver.com/9/27373; Emma Vandore, "Sarkozy, Merkel, Blair Call for New Capitalism," Information Liberation, 17 January 2009, http://www.informationliberation.com/?id=26388; "Capitalism Has to Be Changed, French President Sarkozy says," eTurboNews, 27 January 2010, http://www.eturbonews.com/14078/capitalism-has-be-changed-french-president-sarkozy-says.

11. I do not seek to diminish the significance of financial and innovation-related businesses; to the extent that they play the roles they were initially accorded, they are essential for the modern economy. However, in their current permutations both tend to create "bubbles." The largest price imbalances occur most rapidly in these sectors, and such redistribution of aggregate product has the potential to create a crisis.

12. That distinguishes producers of software from companies using fashion as a marketing factor. Fashion, unlike these "innovations," is not forced upon the consumer.

13. One certainly needs talent to exert such direct influence on consumers—advertising, public relations, and sales talent. But if talent of this kind predominates and is valued more highly than other talents—of engineers and managers—then you can assume that business is heading toward a crisis.

14. I learned from market research specialists (of Russian consumers, but I doubt that the situation in this respect is much different in the West) that some 75 percent of smartphone owners could not correctly answer questions about using their gadgets to perform advanced tasks. More than 70 percent of them answered that manuals for their phones were "too voluminous and difficult to understand," which in effect meant that most users didn't care to use at least a considerable portion of the phones' "innovative features."

15. This notion or allusions to it could be found scattered in thousands of mass media publications or public statements of all sorts of respected and influential people. So I don't consider it proper to single out any names or institutions as main proponents of these ideas.

16. Strictly speaking, Gazprom is not a single corporation but rather a vast business group with complex internal ties and blurred boundaries.

CHAPTER 4: International Relations, 1980s–2008

1. The "Greek crisis" of 2010 can be seen as a manifestation of the change in attitudes toward the issue of gaps in the levels of economic development. Greece insisted that the EU had a responsibility to help close the existing gaps through international financing, whatever might be the costs to more

developed economies. Those countries, however (Germany in particular), have made it clear that the issue of cost is most important and should prevail over the principle of overcoming differences in the standards of living.

2. Developments in Africa could serve as an example: after the end of the Cold War areas of chronic poverty and political instability in this region stopped attracting attention of Western governments, which ceded to international aid organizations the initiative to end famine and curb internal conflicts. Such an abdication of responsibility to organizations that lacked adequate resources and experience led to massacres in Rwanda and Darfur, where hundreds of thousands were murdered or starved to death. Under such conditions pinning hopes on the efficient function of market mechanisms to stimulate manufacturing production in that part of the world amounted to self-deceit and hypocrisy.

3. For example, in the minds of a lot of people in Asia, Africa, Latin America, and eastern Europe, many famous brand names are associated with the "Western way of life," and the natural drive for modernization leads people to drink Coca-Cola rather than demand more respect for human rights or imposition of fair business practices and fair trials in their countries. Owners of trademarks thus are able to charge extra for selling together with their products a portion of the "American dream" (or "European values"), for which they bear no cost.

4. Imagine, for example, an ambitious individual or group—a newcomer from a non-Western country—that aspires to create a large structure offering these services on international markets. Obviously any money invested in such a project would be wasted, as it is simply impossible to buy such things as decades-long (or even centuries-long) history, established and constantly promoted stereotypes, or cultural dominance of the existing world business leaders. I wonder whether the group of influential individuals advancing the extremely costly project of "turning Moscow into a world financial center" sincerely believe in the prospects of this venture. Expectation of the fruits of personal involvement in planning multibillion-dollar project budgets is a more plausible motive.

5. I am ready to admit that the expression "deprived of the chance" may not reflect the situation quite correctly. Historically speaking, many nations may have been given a chance— in some cases more than one—that they failed to use. Nevertheless, as the gap between winners and losers deepens, surmounting the gap becomes progressively difficult, whatever resources those lagging behind devote to this purpose.

6. This gap has been intensified by the crisis, or, rather by the wide-ranging subsidies the crisis forced the developed countries to allocate in order to support their own economies.

7. As Robert Shiller writes (admittedly with respect to capitalism in general): "Capitalism will produce not only what people really want, but also what they think they want. It can produce the medicine people want to cure their

ills. . . . But if it can do so profitably, it will also produce what people mistakenly want. It will produce snake oil. Not only that: it may also produce the want for the snake oil itself" (*Financial Times*, 8 March 2009). When we project this principle onto the international level, less developed countries are the most vulnerable.

8. I could, for example, name some eastern European countries recently admitted to the European Union, or relatively successful Latin American countries like Brazil or Chile. But such a list will certainly be short and quite likely to change if we turn once again to this subject ten or fifteen years from now.

9. It is true that Russia has traits attributable to its specific civilization and culture formed over a thousand years of history that distinguish it from other countries and peoples. However, it is my earnest conviction that these traits should be considered only with respect to the methods and measures required to modernize and reform Russia and the most effective practical implementation of such procedures. They are irrelevant when considering the path that Russia should take or Russia's ultimate form.

10. Official measures to facilitate reforms were accompanied by other no less powerful, and perhaps even more powerful, processes. For example, ever since the second half of the 1990s corruption in Russia has been a constant target of harsh criticism by the Western media and governments. However, we know that corrupt Russian officials do not keep their money in the banks of Fidel Castro or in China. They do not stash all their money in offshore accounts: they also bank it in New York, Zurich, Munich, Paris, and London. The scale of the corruption in Russia would be unthinkable without the cooperation of Western business and representatives of political elites.

11. The most famous and dramatic example concerns the fate of Mikhail Khodorkovsky, whose drama is attributable less to political ambitions or problems in personal relations than to the absolutely opaque, semicriminal privatization of large swaths of property implemented in the 1990s in the style of crony capitalism—and, incidentally, fully supported by Western governments. Like many others, Khodorkovsky was simultaneously a participant in and victim of those processes. The difference is that in his case the financial and political aspects were far more prominent than in other cases that were no less tragic, and frequently far more so. The criminality of the privatization implemented in the 1990s served as an effective tool for blackmail after 2000, with selective punishment of undesirable businessmen and the political suppression of business as a whole.

12. See, for example, Grigory Yavlinsky, "Need to Legitimize Large Private Property in Russia and Ways to Do So: Defining the Problem," *Voprosy Ekonomiki,* no. 9 (2007): 4–26; G. Yavlinsky, "Economic Legitimacy Pact," www.Gazeta.ru, 10 July 2007.

13. The Cox Report of a congressional committee in 2000 on the Russian policy of the Clinton administration stated openly that the United States had not

supported the democratic opposition in Russia, as its support would have
been an admission that Yeltsin was not a democrat and that his policies were
not democratic.

14. The key players, who were publicly and unconditionally supported by the
West, were extremely unpopular with the majority of the Russian population; these people were simply hated in their own country. It does not
matter here whether that hatred was justified or not, though I believe it
was. The salient point is that the West was represented politically in Russia
by unpopular figures.

15. The Russian leadership and "democratic" favorites received more than
moral support. The IMF in effect financed the cruel and bloody war in the
northern Caucasus in 1994–1999 and incited separatism in Abkhazia and
South Ossetia.

16. David Stuckler and Lawrence King from Cambridge University and Martin
McKee from the London School of Hygiene and Tropical Medicine
conducted an analysis of three million men of working age who died in
former communist countries of eastern Europe. The results suggest that
at least a third were victims of mass privatization, which led to widespread
unemployment and social disruption (*Financial Times*, 15 January 2009).

   The study adds to growing research in recent years demonstrating how
far the economic transition led to widespread suffering through death and
physical and mental illness. The research takes a specific swipe at the legacy
of Jeffrey Sachs, the U.S. economist who advocated shock therapy at the
time.

17. Here is a representative quotation from a March 2009 interview with one
of the key players in the early 1990s, acting prime minister and minister of
finance in 1991–1993, Yegor Gaidar: "I believe that in this crisis we were
resolving two key tasks. We wanted to prevent famine, which was an absolute reality, and we wanted to prevent civil war. We coped with both these
tasks."

18. Jeffrey Sachs, interview, 15 March 2005 to discuss his book, http://www
.washingtonpost.com/wp-dyn/articles/A27201-2005Mar11.html.

19. At Davos in 1993 I said in a speech to a group of Western economic
advisers: "There was a custom in prerevolutionary Russia for engineers who
designed railroad bridges to stand under the bridge when the first train went
over it. So if you intend to give advice to Russia, maybe you should move
to Russia with your families to be with the people you are advising, and
experience all the hardships and deprivations stipulated by the plans that you
propose." In late 1992, as the result of a single instantaneous liberalization
of prices (in the course of one day!) in an excessively monopolized state
economy, annual inflation reached 2,600 percent. Some time later the U.S.
Justice Department investigated the activities of a number of the advisers
to Russia. It identified serious abuses, and some of the advisers had to pay
material fines.

20. We have before our eyes the most recent example of the collapse of the Madoff financial empire. He was basically turned in by his own sons.

21. The program of Western assistance to the Soviet Union was aimed to ensure the country's transition to democracy and market economy and its incorporating into global markets. The program was developed in 1991 by the Center for Economic and Political Studies (EPICenter) in cooperation with a group of Western economists. For details see *The Grand Bargain* (New York: Pantheon, 1991).

C H A P T E R 5 : The Crisis in Russia Is a Different Matter

1. If anyone has gotten the impression that the Soviet system was demolished according to some conscious and clever plan, that impression is wrong. The system rather collapsed of its own when Soviet leaders in 1990–1991 left it to its fate, doing nothing to maintain conditions necessary for systematic and orderly preservation or reform. In fact the same economists (like Gaidar) who later presided over its general collapse had warned against the risks of abrupt destruction of the system; they advocated instead a long and smooth transition that would have preserved all the elements of control and regulation that might prove useful and stabilizing. In reality, they implemented the policy of "shock without therapy," which brought about hyperinflation (2,600 percent in 1992) and the collapse of manufacturing production (more than a 50 percent decline in 1992–1994).

2. If it is held that a dictatorship is marked by having a leader not at the top of the power pyramid whose actions are not controlled by anyone else, but who is himself able to control the actions of a network of subordinates, it would be wishful thinking to call the current political system in Russia a dictatorship.

3. Incidentally, I believe that the term *transitional economy* that was frequently used in the 1990s to describe this system is applicable only with a number of caveats and is in general insubstantial, as it does not contain references to the substance or the direction of the assumed transition. The version "quasi-market" (or "administrative-market") economy is also inaccurate, as all existing economic systems are inevitably eclectic and contain contradictory aspects, for example in their administrative structures.

4. To be convinced of the latter, you simply need to look at the state's own medium- and long-term programs from four or five years ago and compare them with reality. Approximately 90 percent of the government's plans in industrial policy, plans to diversify the economy and implement structural improvements, have not been implemented. Naturally, no one had expected such rapid and steady oil price growth, which objectively acted as a disincentive for diversification and reduced the relative profitability of investments in alternative sectors. However, no political will was demonstrated to ensure rigid implementation of planned measures.

CHAPTER 6: Lessons from the Crisis in a Globalized World

1. Jean Baudrillard wrote extensively on the process of consumer value (utility) giving way to "symbolic value." In postmodern society, Baudrillard argues, people do not buy what they need, they buy symbols, "differentiating marks" that serve to identify the consumer as a member of a certain social group. Goods and services which perform the function of a sign, of a symbol, do not satisfy any definite need of a consumer; their only purpose is to identify the consumer as a part of a certain stratum or social group. *Selected Writings* (Stanford: Stanford University Press, 2001).

2. A good example cited by P. J. O'Rourke in the *Financial Times* is provided by Adam Smith's interpretation of the revenue generated from renting a house. While renting the house is a real source of revenue for the home-owner, according to Smith, it does not increase the revenue and prosperity of society as a whole, as it is not economic activity per se, and the money paid by the tenant to the homeowner has to be obtained by the tenant from some other, real activity. "A dwelling-house, as such, contributes nothing to the revenue of its inhabitant," Smith wrote in *The Wealth of Nations*. "If it is let to a tenant for rent, as the house itself can produce nothing, the tenant must always pay the rent out of some other revenue." Although a house can make money for its owner if it is rented, "the revenue of the whole body of the people can never be in the smallest degree increased by it." Quoted in *Financial Times*, 10 February 2009.

3. Globalization has also distorted our moral compass. It has lowered the social and political responsibility of the wealthy, especially people living in one country but making money from another. The criteria of public reputation are flouted as the quality of politics deteriorates at almost every level. The mix of cultures has also generated a number of complex behavioral effects. For example, we have witnessed the appearance of cultural factors that may have affected the concept of being true to one's word. According to the tradition of certain political and business elites, especially post-Soviet, irresponsibility is virtually a norm of life, while one's word is simply ritual. If you hear the word "yes," you should be ready to accept that this may simply be a form of politeness and is devoid of all meaning. The widespread dissemination of such cultural attitudes has proved extremely destructive.

4. Special drawing rights, a form of international money, created by the International Monetary Fund, and defined as a weighted average of various convertible currencies, could be used by IMF member countries as a reserve currency and as a means of covering international trade balance deficits and repaying international debt.

5. *Woe from Wit* (1828). Griboyedov (1795–1829), a Russian playwright, poet, diplomat, and composer, was head of the Russian diplomatic mission to Iran, all of whom were murdered in Tehran by a crowd of religious fanatics.

6. We must not underestimate the historical importance of the Universal Declaration of Human Rights adopted by the U.N. General Assembly on 10 December 1948. The effort by the United Nations to publicize the text of the declaration and "to cause it to be disseminated, displayed, read, and expounded principally in schools and other educational institutions" could play an essential role in nurturing a generation of leaders who would not only learn the values established by this declaration but come to embody them.

Conclusion

1. *Euronews,* 7 May 2010.
2. Again, Jacques Attali: "The crisis started out being small American sub-primes which should have cost 10 billion dollars, but nothing was done and it became a global banking crisis which could have cost 500 billion dollars . . . but again nothing was done except passing it onto the taxpayers. It has become a national debt crisis which now totals between 7 and 8 trillion dollars." *Euronews,* 7 May 2010.

BIBLIOGRAPHY

Ahamed, Liaquat. *Lords of Finance: The Bankers Who Broke the World*. New York: Penguin, 2009.

Akerlof, George. A., and Robert J. Schiller. *Animal Spirits: How Human Psychology Drives the Economy, and Why It Matters for Global Capitalism*. Princeton: Princeton University Press, 2009.

Allison, Graham, and Grigory Yavlinsky, eds. *Window of Opportunity: The Grand Bargain for Democracy in the Soviet Union*. New York: Pantheon, 1991.

Attali, Jacques. *A Brief History of the Future: A Brave and Controversial Look at the Twenty-First Century*. Trans. Jeremy Leggatt. 2006; New York: Arcade, 2009.

Bernstein, Peter L. *Capital Ideas Evolving*. Hoboken, N.J.: Wiley. 2009.

Buzgalin, A. V., ed. *Transformatsionnaia ekonomika Rossii* [Transformational economy of Russia]. Moscow: Finansy i statistika, 2006.

Cohan, William D. *House of Cards: A Tale of Hubris and Wretched Excess on Wall Street*. New York: Doubleday, 2009.

Cooper, George. *The Origin of Financial Crises: Central Banks, Credit Bubbles, and the Efficient Market Fallacy*. New York: Vintage, 2008.

Einhorn, David. *Fooling Some of the People All of the Time: A Long Short Story*. Updated and rev. Wiley, 2008.

Fleckenstein, William A. *Greenspan's Bubbles: The Age of Ignorance at the Federal Reserve*. New York: McGraw-Hill, 2008.

Gaddis, John Lewis. *The Cold War: A New History*. New York: Penguin, 2005.

Galbraith, James K. *The Predator State: How Conservatives Abandoned the Free Market and Why Liberals Should Too*. New York: Free Press, 2008.

Gilman, Martin. *Defolt, kotorogo moglo i ne byt'* [The default that could have been avoided]. Moscow: Vremya, 2009.

Gilpin, Robert, with the assistance of Jean Millis Gilpin. *The Challenge of Global Capitalism: The World Economy in the 21st Century*. Princeton: Princeton University Press, 2002.

Grant, James. *Mr. Market Miscalculates: The Bubble Years and Beyond*. Edinburg, Va.: Axios, 2008.

Greenspan, Alan. *The Age of Turbulence: Adventures in a New World*. New York: Penguin, 2008.

Klein, Naomi. *No Logo: No Space, No Choice, No Jobs.* New York: Picador, 2002.

———. *The Shock Doctrine: The Rise of Disaster Capitalism.* New York: Picador, 2008.

Krugman, Paul. *The Conscience of a Liberal.* New York: Norton, 2007.

———. *The Great Unraveling: Losing Our Way in the New Century.* New York: Norton, 2004.

———. *The Return of Depression Economics and the Crisis of 2008.* New York: Norton, 2009.

Lewis, Michael, ed. *Panic: The Story of Modern Financial Insanity.* New York: Norton, 2009.

———, ed. *The Real Price of Everything: Rediscovering the Six Classics of Economics.* Sterling, 2008.

Mau, Vladimir. *Institutsional'nye predposylki sovremennogo ekonomicheskogo rosta* [Institutional prerequisites for modern economic growth]. Moscow: IEPP, 2007.

Minsky, Hyman. *Stabilizing an Unstable Economy.* McGraw-Hill, 2008.

Morris, Charles R. The Two Trillion Dollar Meltdown: Easy Money, High Rollers, and the Great Credit Crash. New York: Public Affairs, 2009.

Muolo, Paul, and Matthew Padilla. *Chain of Blame: How Wall Street Caused the Mortgage and Credit Crisis.* Hoboken, N.J.: Wiley, 2008.

Phillips, Kevin. *Bad Money: Reckless Finance, Failed Politics, and the Global Crisis of American Capitalism.* New York: Penguin, 2009.

Reich, Robert B. *Supercapitalism: The Transformation of Business, Democracy, and Everyday Life.* New York: Vintage, 2008.

Sachs, Jeffrey. *Common Wealth: Economics for a Crowded Planet.* New York: Penguin, 2009.

———. *The End of Poverty: Economic Possibilities for Our Time.* New York: Penguin, 2006.

Schiller, Robert J. *The Subprime Solution: How Today's Global Financial Crisis Happened and What to Do about It.* Princeton: Princeton University Press, 2008.

Smick, David M. *The World Is Curved: Hidden Dangers to the Global Economy.* New York: Portfolio, 2008.

Soros, George. *The New Paradigm for Financial Markets: The Credit Crisis of 2008 and What It Means.* New York: Public Affairs, 2008.

Stiglitz, Joseph E. *Globalization and Its Discontents.* New York: Norton, 2003.

———. *Making Globalization Work.* New York: Norton, 2007.

Taylor, John B. *Getting Off Track: How Government Actions and Interventions Caused, Prolonged, and Worsened the Financial Crisis.* Stanford: Hoover Institution Press, 2009.

Wolf, Martin. *Fixing Global Finance.* Baltimore: Johns Hopkins University Press, 2008.

Woods, Thomas E., Jr. *Meltdown: A Free-Market Look at Why the Stock Market*

Collapsed, the Economy Tanked, and Government Bailouts Will Make Things Worse. Washington, D.C.: Regnery, 2009.

Yankelovich, Daniel. *Profit with Honor: The New Stage of Market Capitalism*. Yale University Press, 2007.

Yavlinsky, Grigory. *Demodernizatsiia* [Demodernisation]. Moscow: Epicenter, 2002.

———. *Laissez-Faire versus Policy-Led Transformation: Lessons of the Economic Reforms in Russia*. Moscow: Epicenter, 1994.

———. *Periferiinyi kapitalizm* [Peripheral capitalism]. Moscow: Epicenter, 2003.

———. *Perspektivy Rossii. Ekonomicheskii i politicheskii vzgliad* [Russia's prospects: An economic and political view]. Moscow: Galleia-print, 2006.

———. *Rossiiskaia ekonomicheskaia sistema: Nastoiashchee i budushchee* [The Russian economic system: Today and tomorrow]. Moscow: Medium, 2007.

———. "Russia's Phony Capitalism." *Foreign Affairs* 77 (1998): 67–79.

Yavlinsky, Grigory, and Serguey Braguinsky. *Incentives and Institutions: The Transition to a Market Economy in Russia*. Princeton: Princeton University Press, 2000.

———. "The Inefficiency of Laissez-Faire in Russia: Hysteresis Effects and the Need for Policy-Led Transformation." *Journal of Comparative Economics*. 19 (1994): 88–116.

———. *Stimuly i instituty: Perekhod k rynochnok ekonomike v Rossii* [Incentives and institutions: The transition to a market economy in Russia]. Moscow: GU VShE, 2007.

Yavlinsky, Grigory, et al. *500 Days: Transition to the Market Economy*. Ed. David Kushner. New York: St. Martin's, 1991.

ACKNOWLEDGMENTS

This book was initiated by Jonathan Brent, who commissioned it for Yale University Press in 2008. He persuaded me to write it after our conversations about the financial crisis. Jonathan was with me every step of the way, and all his remarks and suggestions were invariably useful.

I am infinitely grateful to the outstanding professional Dr. Vitaly Shvydko and to the brilliant scholar Victor Kogan-Yasny for many years of discussion and debate that strengthened my convictions and helped me formulate my ideas in a clear way. Their encouragement and professional collaboration meant a great deal to me and gave me enormous personal support.

I would like to thank my old friends Antonina and Jean-Claude Bouis for the care with which they reviewed the original manuscript. The sensitive translation by Antonina W. Bouis conveys both the meaning and spirit of my text. Jean-Claude was characteristically generous in providing me with his thoughtful and creative comments in the course of his analytical editing of the book.

My thanks go to Professor Serguey Braguinsky for finding the time to read my book and to give me advice that kept it moving on track.

The thoughtful political analyst Andrei Kosmynin and my Russian editor Yuri Zdorovov read the manuscript in its early stages and made valuable suggestions.

I would also like to thank Eugenia Dillendorf, who read the book with extraordinary care and helped me in every conceivable way.

I am grateful to the team at Yale University Press—Sarah Miller, who attentively shepherded the book, and Dan Heaton, whose copyediting was an important learning experience for me.

Basil Ballhatchet did important stylistic work on an early draft, and I thank him for his time and commitment. I also thank Olga Radayeva, who unfailingly handled every problem that came up over the past two years in the course of preparing the book for publication.

As always, the main inspiration of my life is my wife, Elena. My brother, Mikhail Yavlinsky, and his family created the conditions for me to work on this book. For that and much more, my eternal gratitude.

This book would not exist without you all.

G.Y.

Moscow, May 17, 2011

INDEX

Abkhazia, 151*n*15
advertising: business journalism as, 55; consumers manipulated by, 6, 52, 56, 126; cost of, 65–66; globalization and, 67, 73, 82, 84; technologically advanced, 51. *See also* consumer needs; marketing
Afghanistan, 100, 102
American International Group (AIG), 16, 127
appeasement, 41
arbitrage, 69
Arthur Andersen, 44
Attali, Jacques, 138
auditing, 44, 59, 82, 83, 85
Australia, 17, 86
authoritarianism, 7, 94, 97, 113, 121, 141

"bad debts," 18
bailouts, 46, 105, 138
balance of trade, 63
Balkans, 101
Bank of America, 43
bankruptcy, 12, 16, 20, 23, 104
Baudrillard, Jean, 124
biotechnology, 72
black market, 7
Blair, Tony, 71
blocs-building policy, 132, 134
bonuses, 33, 46–47, 125
Bosnia, 100
branding, 51, 66
Brazil, 17

bribery, 38, 100, 112
brokerage, 53–54
bubbles, 20, 21, 25, 54, 58, 120
bureaucracy, 91, 94, 95, 108, 113, 115, 117
Burma (Myanmar), 101
Bush, George H. W., 133
Bush, George W., 22, 98
business cycle, 2, 19; taming of, 20–21
business services, 49, 52

Canada, 17
"capitalism of production," 31–32
Cassano, Joseph J., 127
Cayman Islands, 58–59
Chechnya, 132
China, 50, 51, 88, 89–90
Clinton, Bill, 98
coercion, 38–39, 109–110
Cold War, 27, 30, 89, 101, 102, 131, 133
collateralized debt obligations, 42
commission system, 43
commodities, 21, 86; prices of, 17, 23, 116, 119–120
comparative advantage, 50
competition, 40
computer technology, 65, 72
confidence, 37–38
conflict of civilizations, 7, 104
consumer lending, 61–64
consumer needs, 4, 7, 50, 56, 60, 67, 124. *See also* advertising